The Trusting Time

A Collection of Christian Poetry

Jodie Mitchell

Patsy,
May you always
Trust God for His strength
during your own Trusting Time!!!
He is Timeless!!!
Ecc 3:11
:)
Jodie
Mitchell

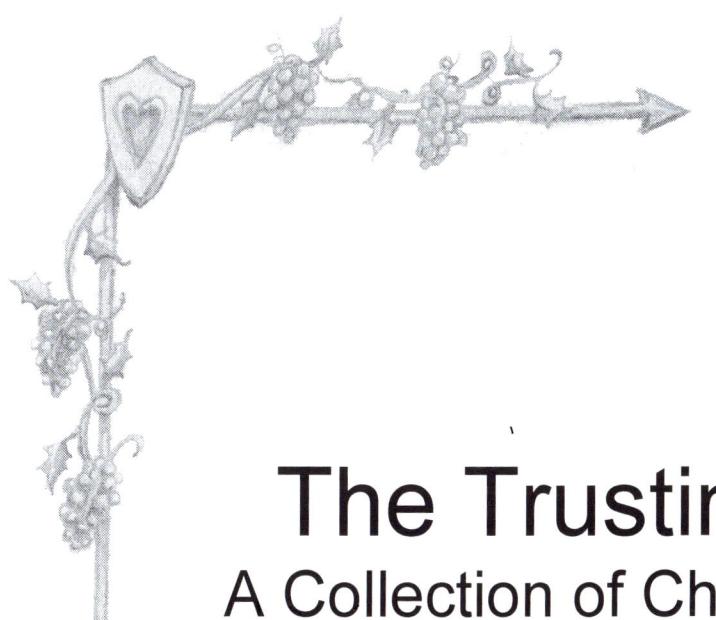

Copyright © 2011 Jodie Mitchell. All rights reserved.

No part of this publication's content may be reproduced, stored in a retrieval system, or transmitted in any form or by any means---electronic, mechanical, photocopy, recording, or any other---without the prior permission of the Author.

Unless otherwise indicated, all Scripture references are from THE HOLY BIBLE, NEW INTERNATIONAL VERSION®, NIV® Copyright © 1973, 1978, 1984, 2011 by Biblica, Inc.™ Used by permission. All rights reserved worldwide.

ISBN: 1463780796
ISBN-13: 978-1463780791

Printed in the United States of America
by CreateSpace

DEDICATION

This book is dedicated to my Loving Husband Philip Mitchell. God has blessed me so much by his Spiritual Leadership and by him being a true example of what it means for a husband to love his wife the way Christ Loves the Church.

Soul Mate from Heaven

The sweet words you say, words of Love and Care,
Are sweeter even still when you say them in a prayer.

The way you treat others when you are so kind,
Shows the brightest reflection of a Christ like mind.

Our romantic moments with soft music heard,
Becomes more valuable, when studying God's word.

And though roses are beautiful and candy is sweet,
Christ in our marriage is what makes it complete.

So it would not be unthinkable or sound very odd,
When I say your love brings me closer to God.

And that is why, I have always believed from the start,
That you are my soul mate, sent from God's Heart.

The Trusting Time

TABLE OF CONTENTS

Dedication	....	iii
Acknowledgments	....	ix
Introduction	....	xiii

Chapter 1	Autograph of Love	....	1
Chapter 2	The Heart Mender	....	19
Chapter 3	Expressions	....	41
Chapter 4	The Power of Prayer	....	55
Chapter 5	View From the Top	....	71
Chapter 6	The Trusting Time	....	87
Chapter 7	Take Another Look America	......	123
Chapter 8	More Than Stories	....	135
Chapter 9	Simple Poems	....	149
Chapter 10	Just A Kid	....	163
Chapter 11	The Gift of Christmas	....	183
Chapter 12	Have You Seen Jesus?	....	195

One Last Plea	....	214
An Invitation for You	....	216
(P.S.)	....	219
Alphabetical Index of Poems	....	225
About the Author	....	231

The Trusting Time

ACKNOWLEDGMENTS

Acknowledgement of His Glory

Dear Lord each poem I write, is to acknowledge You,
With the words of many, or sometimes few.
And some of the words, may not rhyme well,
But all have the same story to tell.
Of how much You love and value, the human man,
And how we can all be a part of Your Plan.
And now I want to take this time to let You know,
How very thankful I am, for You loving me so.
And thank you for my talent, that You've given to me,
So I can minister to others, by this poetry.
For these poems are not to reach, any public fame,
But only to proclaim, Thy Holy Name.
And these poems are not special, unless they are inspired,
By My Lord of whom I most admire.
So in giving You all the glory, use these poems I sincerely pray,
So that whoever reads them, will be touched by You today.

I would like to express my sincerest gratitude to all of my family, friends and others along the way who have helped to encourage, challenge and inspire me to display my writings in the form of a book.

I would also like to personally thank:

Emily Young
For the cover photo and photos in chapters 1,4,6,8,9,10

Phil Mitchell
For the photos in chapters 2,3,5,7,11

June Dagnell
For the photo in chapter 12

A very special thank you to:

Julia Richardson
For all of the Illustrations

The talent of all these artists have helped capture and complement the poetry in this book.

INTRODUCTION

The poems within the pages of this book started many years ago when I was just a young girl, who like any other girl at the age of eleven was shy, insecure and trying to discover what life was all about. So, with pen and paper I wrote poetry to express myself, my life experiences and my heart for God.

I learned early on the importance of how an individual needs Jesus in order to find their place in the world and how much dependence on God is required once that place in this world is found.

I have experienced much pain and disappointment from people who have let me down, often at the most important times in my life when I needed someone to be there. Yet, having entrusted my life to Jesus, I have also learned that those difficult times often led me to see more of a Savior who would never leave me, forsake me or dishearten me in any way. I have discovered more and more each day just how much I need Jesus to walk with me, lead me and teach me His Ways.

Long before this book became a reality, trusting God and His timing were essential to me growing and becoming more of who God wanted me to be as a Christ follower. I have kept record of many of those moments through the poems you will read in each chapter.

No matter where you are in your journey with God, there are two truths that are inescapable. God is Trustworthy. God is Timeless. It doesn't matter who you are, where you are going or what you will do, these two truths hold a very simple yet serious message.

This book is about a Savior, a Cross and a Connection that He wants to make with each of us which will continue throughout eternity. God wants YOU to trust Him and let Him set your life according to His Divine time.

There is something in this book for everyone. There are poems that will encourage the single heart, the prayerful heart and the thankful heart. Poems that point to God's creation, calm us in our troubles, celebrate Christ in our traditions and remind us how we need God in our country. There is even a chapter that can be read to children or help you rekindle past memories of your own childhood.

However, I have reserved the last chapter of this book, Chapter 12 "Have You Seen Jesus" as an important invitation for anyone who would like to know Christ or for those who would like to share their faith with others.

Furthermore, please don't miss out on two important features of this book that deserve your attention. These features are to me, as inspirational as the poems themselves.

The first feature is at the end of each chapter where I have listed scripture references for selected poems from that chapter. These will help you understand where my inspiration for the poems originated from and give you an opportunity for your own personal study and time in God's Word.

The second feature is called "P.S.", which is located at the back of the book. Here you will find inside information about the poems, such as the title of my first poem, which poems were recently written, why I wrote certain poems and a few other interesting details about me and how this book came to be. Inside each tidbit of information is a morsel for you to enjoy as a "Backstage Pass" to what God was doing each time I picked up my pen and wrote.

These small yet largely relevant times in my writing career hopefully will help you gain knowledge of some of my most treasured writing experiences and also help you to reflect on how God is present around YOU and wants to use YOUR gifts and talents for His Glory, whatever they may be.

This book "The Trusting Time" that you hold in your hands, is not by accident or coincidence. Every title, phrase, photograph and border of elegance, is more than just creative rhymes and rhythms of poetry. Each and every detail has been planned strategically to drive home the theme of trust and time and by reading the entire book, you will walk away with more than what you first anticipated from a poetry book.

So, if you haven't already, pull up a chair and pour a cup of your favorite beverage, start anywhere in this book and enjoy! Oh, and don't forget to pause every once in a while and say a prayer to God for Jesus to be the answer for your own heart, your own life and your own "Trusting Time".

Jodie Mitchell

This is love: not that we loved God, but that he loved us and sent his Son as an atoning sacrifice for our sins.

I John 4:10

CHAPTER ONE

AUTOGRAPH OF LOVE

Autograph of Love

At the beginning of my life so dark and gray,
A famous author held me in strife, because I couldn't pay.

A debt of living a life of sin, could not be taken back,
So this author took his pen and wrote his name in black.

For many years I felt the grief, of the poison of his name,
And so I continued in unbelief, of ever releasing my shame.

Then the news reached my ears, of Hope to set me free,
A New Author was now here but what could He do for me?

My life was in the dark of night, my soul was bound for hell,
It would take Heavens Light to break through this prison cell.

Yet, this New Author felt my pain, when He saw Guilty in its evil art,
So, He reached out His Living vein and wrote Forgiven upon my heart.

Now I sing and now I dance I'm living proof you see,
Of one who has been given a second chance, for all Eternity.

This New Author who loves us all, gives me a Joy from above,
He has written Jesus name upon my heart, with His autograph of Love.

A Savior's Love for You

Experience the softness, of the petals so red,
Remember the Savior, whose blood for us was shed.

Experience the long stem, of the single red rose,
Remember the length, of Calvary's road.

Experience the thorns, they are sharp with pain,
Remember the Savior, His dying was our gain.

Experience this rose, its beauty so new,
As you remember, the Savior's Love for you.

Coronation at Calvary

An arrangement had been made,
And the crowd was getting restless,
For the sight they had waited to see.

A proclamation was announced,
And a declaration pronounced,
It was a welcoming for a King.

A crown and robe was prepared,
As the crowd began to stare,
And the successor stepped forth to be received.

But no loud and joyful cheering,
For this royalty appearing,
Only mocking and disputing were to be.

Then a parade began to form,
On their way up to the throne,
That had been provided for the King.

But no rejoicing and adoring,
Could be found in this morning,
As they held it on a hill, called Calvary.

For no one believed that He was the King,
For the ceremony about to take place.

They showed hate and rejection,
For this royal reception,
Death was the honor He would face.

So they nailed Him to a cross,
In which they called His throne,
And spectators just stood
And watched Him bleed.

And we were all there,
In this tragedy we share,
At the coronation that was held...
For you and me.

Even the Flowers Knew

One day many years ago, clouds filled the sky,
Darkness hovered over all the earth, when Jesus was crucified.
Birds that sang such pretty songs, could not sing out a tune,
For even the beautiful flowers knew and so they did not bloom.

Rushing waters that filled the streams, suddenly were still,
Grass began to wither, upon the greenest hills,
Life itself had become extinct and begin to fade,
For the joy and peace of God was buried where Jesus laid.

But though it seemed Love was lost and all Hope was gone,
The sun started breaking through, to bring a brand new dawn.
For Jesus Christ had risen and elation filled the air,
The trees rejoiced with gladness and peace was everywhere.

For the birds were restored their singing, life was fresh as spring,
The hills exclaimed the victory, to every living thing.
The flowers sprang out in every color, filling every space,
For life had been touched by the Hands of God, by His wonderful Grace.

And the miracle reached to every stream and every oceans shore,
For Jesus Christ is yesterday, today and forevermore.

Heaven's Love

Many years ago, a follower named John,
Went baptizing people by night and by dawn.
He said I baptize thee with water, but I shall not boast,
Because Jesus will baptize you, with the Holy Ghost.

Then one day Jesus, was baptized by John,
And the heavens were opened, and filled with sweet song,
And the Spirit like a dove had descended down,
Suddenly, a voice from heaven broke through with great sound.

The voice was Jesus' Father, whose voice spoke with ease,
"Thou art my beloved Son, in whom I am well pleased."
This I am sure would have been something to see,
Something in which heaven's love could only bring to be.

Love Throughout the Ages

This is a celebration of your time together,
Special memories to share and to hold forever,
Reminders of love are around us tonight,
Everything looks beautiful with soft candlelight.

And though life is unexpected of what it takes us through,
It's God's Love through the ages that preserves me and you.
The love that comes from our hearts with tenderness and care,
Keeps its strength and beauty because of One so fair.

The joy of our loving hearts are filled with such elation,
Because of One broken heart that offers us salvation.
Romantic songs of love capture sweet melody
But none are quite as sweet as "Amazing Grace", you see.

For it is Christ's Love for the church, whose blood has stained the pages,
Of time and centuries that have passed, with Love throughout the ages.

My Wedding Day

I have been a part of weddings many times before,
When the bride and groom are joined as one forevermore.

And I too want to be married when that day finally comes,
When the groom wants me as His chosen one.

But I'm not referring to the one on earth you see,
I'm waiting for the marriage of Holy Unity.

When my Savior will call the Church His bride,
And we will always live with Him at His side.

Just think of what the beautiful reception will bring,
For the Royal Bride and her Groom the King.

All will stand in awe as we enter in Heaven's place,
Adorned in His Majesty because we're saved by grace.

And as angels sing songs His Love we will proclaim,
As we rejoice eternally gathered in His Name.

Never Thirst Again

There came a lonely woman, to draw water from the well,
Her heart was filled with sorrow; her life was bound for hell.

The Lord said to the woman drink my water; I am your friend,
This water is everlasting, you will never thirst again.

Drink of the Water, the well will not run dry,
Drink of the Water, it saves so many lives.

For when you drink of the Water, God frees you from your sin,
Oh, drink of the Water and never thirst again.

Are you like this woman, who at first could only see?
A well of earthly water that one day would not be.

If so, then come to Jesus; don't wait until the end,
He has the Living Water, so you shall never thirst again.

Shadows

After Jesus had walked many days on the earth, the day had finally arrived.
The moment He would die, to save so many lives.

I saw in the shadows on the ground, all my darkened sin,
Now, they were upon my Lord... in a place where I should have been.

And as the sun disappeared as if it were the night,
I saw shadows once again fall across the sky...

In anguish and shame of what was revealed to me,
I prayed for my forgiveness and God did set me free.

And it was then I realized, just how great the cost,
For then I saw... only one shadow left... the Shadow of the Cross.

Taking a Moment

In life's busy moments, we all must slip away,
And think of a more perfect place, that we shall see one day.

At times when we are stuck in traffic, we need to interrupt,
This moment of confusion, by lifting our eyes up.

For all the problems of this world, that makes up our daily grind,
Need a break with thoughts from Heaven, to give us peace of mind.

Because one day we will all be home, and Jesus will be there,
And it's time to get excited, for that day is drawing near.

So let us take a moment, away from this world's cruelty,
And concentrate on Heaven, where we'll spend eternity.

The Crucifixion

There once was a man who was arrested, but no wrong did He do.
He was tried and found innocent, But He still died for you.
The cruel roman soldiers, placed a crown of thorns on His head,
"Every king needs a crown", is what the soldiers said.

Then they gave Him a cross to carry, for it was part of the deal,
And they put a robe upon Him, and led Him to the hill.
They nailed Him to the cross, just to watch Him bleed,
They mocked Him, they pierced His side, and smote Him with a reed.

He could have called ten thousand angels, to come down from the sky,
But He stayed upon the cross, for you He chose to die.
Then about the sixth to the ninth hour, there was no sun,
And He cried with a loud voice, "Father! It is done."

They laid Him in a tomb and thought it was the end,
But He arose from the grave, and started living again.
He's living up in heaven somewhere in the blue,
He died and went through all of this, because He loves you.

The Heavenly King

What kind of King would come down to earth? And in a manger lay,
The KING who will bring great things, yet many turn Him away.
What kind of King would reject all of earth's money fame and power?
The KING who healed the lepers, in their needed hour.

What kind of King would ride in town, on a donkey of disgrace?
The KING who wipes away the tears, off every crying face.
What kind of King would in service, wash His disciples feet?
The KING that let roman soldiers, His back badly beat.

What kind of King that being innocent, would on a cross die?
The KING who suffered death, for sinners such as I.

What kind of King would be buried in a tomb, He borrowed from a friend?
The KING that arose from the grave, and is now living again.

What kind of King will one day return, and all shall cry out His name?
JESUS CHRIST the HEAVENLY KING, FOREVER HE SHALL REIGN.

The Main Attraction

When I get to Heaven, it will be so nice,
To enter the pearly gates, which are worth great price.

And when I walk on streets of gold, how lovely they will be,
But even this will not compare, to Heaven's specialty.

For Heaven's main attraction, will still be at hand,
When I join with all the others, and I proudly stand.

To sing praises to our King, with the angels choir,
For this is what I long for, and I most desire.

It will be fine to see the River of Life,
And Tree of Knowledge, standing tall,

But when I lay my eyes on Jesus,
That will be the greatest sight of all,

For a place like Heaven would not exist, if Jesus wasn't there,
With His Light shining Radiance, or His beauty fair.

And even if His home was not Heaven, it would not matter to me,
For Jesus is the only part of Heaven, I truly want to see.

The Snowy Surface

Today the skiers ski with delight,
Racing down the mountains so white,

Leaving their tracks in the crisp snow,
Sliding, gliding or falling as they go.

The tracks and marks in every detail,
Are left by those who have skied the trail.

But at the end of the day when the sun goes down,
Only a used mountain will be found.

The mountain is now ugly the snow grey,
All of its beauty has been skied away.

But later in the night the snow will again fall,
As it covers every scar left by them all.

And just as the snow covers again,
Christ blood can cover your darkest sin.

If your life is scarred by mistakes in your life,
Let the Power of His Love remove all your strife.

Surely as the mountain was restored anew,
So Christ will also do for you.

Yesterday's Miracle

On the first Easter morning, we are all told,
How something miraculous, began to unfold.
For a tomb was left empty, and a stone was rolled away,
And people were amazed, and still even today.

For you see a Man came to die for everyone,
And He was nailed to a cross; He was called God's Son.
And roman soldiers tortured Him, until He reached His doom,
And when He had died, they placed Him in a tomb.

But as history revealed, they found in their despair,
A tomb in which Jesus, was no longer there.
However, there are some, who refuse to face,
That yesterday's miracle, even took place.

Some call it a phenomenon; some call it a lie,
Scientists say that He never really died.
Others say His body was stolen, by His family and friends,
But, for me the mystery has come to an end.

For I believe, from proof, of once living in strife,
That what others may call a mystery, I can call MY LIFE.
And all the untrue sayings, can forever depart,
Because Jesus lives inside my heart.

Scripture References for Selected Poems
Chapter 1
AUTOGRAPH OF LOVE

Autograph of Love	I John 4:10
A Savior's Love for You	John 3:16
Coronation at Calvary	Mark 15: 1-32
Even the Flowers Knew	Hebrews 13:8
Heaven's Love	Luke 3: 15-22
Love Throughout the Ages	Jude 25
My Wedding Day	Revelation 19:7
Never Thirst Again	John 4: 7-15
Shadows	Romans 8: 1-3
Taking a Moment	2 Corinthians 4:18
The Crucifixion	John Chapter 19
The Heavenly King	Psalm 24: 7-10
The Main Attraction	Revelation 21: 21-27, 22: 1-5
The Snowy Surface	Isaiah 1:18
Yesterday's Miracle	I Corinthians 15: 18-31

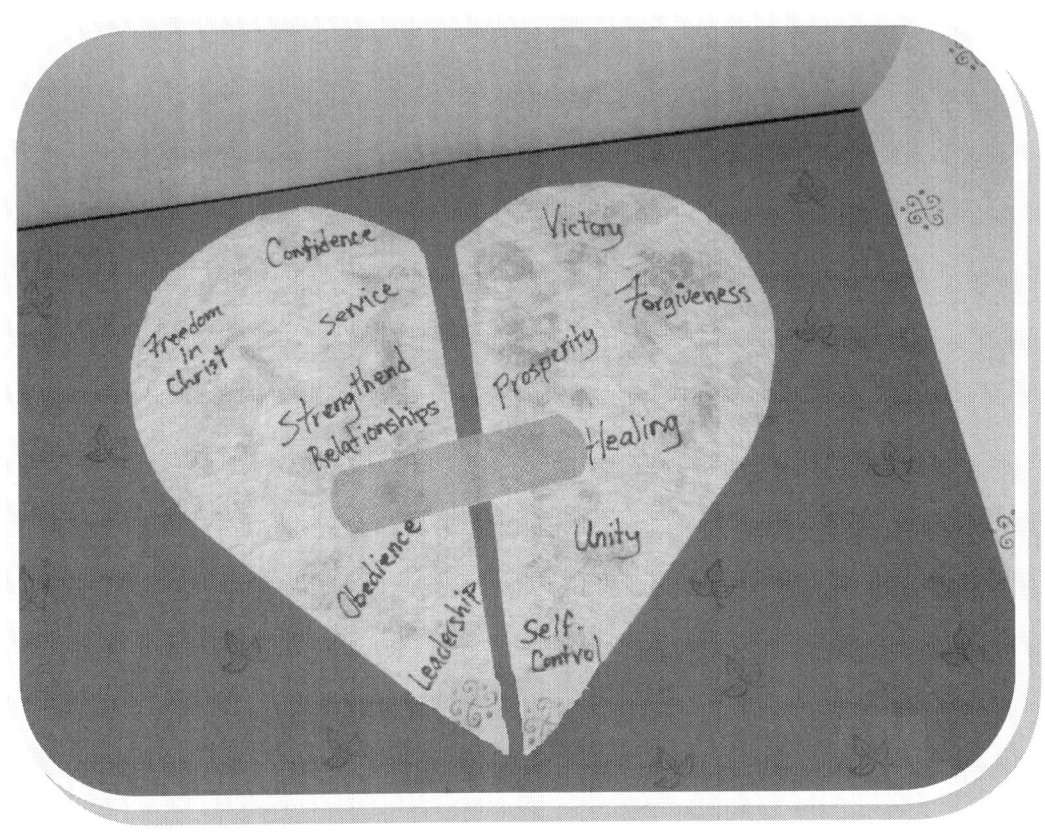

The LORD is close to the brokenhearted and saves those who are crushed in spirit.

Psalm 34:18

CHAPTER TWO
THE HEART MENDER

The Heart Mender

I was floating on cloud nine, not a shadow was mine,
Feeling ten times above,

For what started by chance, was turning into a romance,
I thought I was falling in love.

My heart was singing a song, not a thing was going wrong,
But suddenly things began to change.

I started to cry, I wanted to die,
Everything was re-arranged.

I was so sad and felt very bad,
Feeling like I had been used.

For everything I planned, had slipped out of my hand,
And left me so confused.

So I became very hard as I put up my guard,
To escape all the heartache I had found.

I ran away in fear, with my eyes full of tears,
Leaving my broken heart on the ground.

I was hurting so inside, but there was nowhere to hide,
Away from all of my misery.

But then a voice gave me hope and strength in which to cope,
When it said "lift up your broken heart to me".

At once I felt a peace, all my sadness was released,
Just by meeting this new found friend.

For He picked up my heart that had been torn apart,
And restored it to a whole heart again.

Jesus is the Heart Mender, to Him my life I surrender,
And in my heart His love will always stay.

And now I want to share all His love and His care,
To other broken hearts along the way.

A Change of Heart

Once there was a lonely heart who was sad and blue
Who met up with a loving heart with words of "I Love You".

Then they became a couple's heart, full of happiness,
Until one day the cold heart showed no thoughtfulness.

Then the broken heart began to feel great pain,
And so it seemed now that no heart at all remained.

But God looked down on the empty heart and filled it with sweet love,
And it became a single heart serving Him above.

You see sometimes we don't understand the problems of the heart,
But that's when God is telling us that we've been set apart.

When He allows our closed heart to be broken in two,
In order to make an open heart for His Light to shine through.

For God wants the restless heart to be submissive to His Will,
To create the perfect heart so His Plan He can fulfill.

So let us show a happy heart where everyone can see,
The very, very special heart God's given you and me.

Astray

Oh Lord, we wander, like little sheep astray,
When we lose faith in You, and wander away.
We seem to rely, on things of the wrong,
Like people and friends, that will one day be gone.

When we do wander away, we think You don't care,
But we are so far gone; we don't realize You're there.
I guess if we were to stay, in Your guiding Light,
Then You would seem closer, every day and night.

Yet in those times we don't always understand,
So sometimes we fail, to reach your guiding hand,
Help us to move forward and start fresh again,
As we grow closer to You and further from sin.

A Single Red Rose

A single red rose blooming so fair,
Is often sent by someone who cares.
And in past I waited to receive,
A single red rose sent just for me.

With all of its meaning of joy and love,
Wrapped up in what dreams are truly made of.
And little by little, my world fell apart,
For there was never a rose sent just from the heart.

So I would grow sad day after day,
Because I longed to be loved in a special way.
Until one day, I heard a tender voice,
Telling me that I was His choice.

Making me feel alive once more,
By giving me so much than what I had before.
And to my disbelief of a surprise so sweet,
A single red rose was there at my feet.

But this was no ordinary red rose I found.
For when I picked it up off of the ground,
I noticed it had fallen from a cross standing tall.
Yes, this was a special red rose, after all.

While admiring the beauty of the rose that morn,
My fingers also found the pricks of its thorns.
And it was then that I realized how much suffering and pain,
Had bought my life with a price in which love would remain.

God sent the rose to me and the Rose was His Son,
And from that day on my life had begun.
For JESUS is to me that Single Red Rose,
And forever in my heart is where His Love grows.

Beautiful Lullaby

When I am lonely and broken,
I am comforted by words unspoken.
When I am desolate and have nowhere to go,
There is One who still loves me so.

When I am sinful and full of shame,
There is One who calls me by name.
When I've been betrayed and misled,
There is One who lifts my head.

He calms me with His quiet presence,
Within His arms I find acceptance.
My sleepless nights I find remedy,
In the sound of His endless melody.

As God sings over me throughout the night,
I sleep ever soundly by His touch of moonlight.
In every confidence and through every fear,
He's holding my hand and I can sometimes hear…

The rustle of angels wings when God is near by
As over me he sings a beautiful lullaby.

Blessing Before Bitterness

My heart has been ripped out,
I understand what pain is about,
Once my depression was at its worse.

What happened to me was unfair,
So I fell into great despair,
Believing that love was just a curse.

For I have been treated so mean and cruel,
When I was obeying all the rules,
And I just couldn't understand...

How someone could be so heartless and bold,
To leave my love out in the cold,
When I had never made any demands.

So harboring bitterness deep inside,
With anger and hate to the Lord I cried,
"I will never forgive them for what they've done".

But Jesus quickly reminded me,
Of what a Christian is supposed to be,
And how we are to live as an example for everyone.

I told Him, "Lord it's hard to accept,
When promises made were not kept,"
But He said, "Show them Love"...

"By giving them blessings like I've given you,
No matter what they put you through,
For this is what pleases your Father above".

Commitment of Love

One night I had a talk with my Lord,
And told Him that I was very bored...
Of being in relationships filled with despair,
Often wondering if someone really cared.

For I believe there are no doubts of what to do,
When you find that special love that you know is true.
I wanted someone willing to commit to me,
Not just for the moment but for an eternity.

I would like someone to show me love in a special way,
Not just flatter me with sweet words they might say.
I want to always be a very important part,
Of that certain person's loving heart.

But later I began to gradually find out,
The commitment of love that I had been talking about,
Was exactly what Jesus had been wanting from me...
And I knew that it wasn't what it should be.

For He also expects a love true and real,
Living my life for Him according to God's Will.
Wanting more of my time and more of myself,
Giving all to Him until nothing is left.

Forgiveness of His Own

Have you made a mistake lately in your recent past?
At a time when things were moving way too fast.
Or maybe there is a problem deep down in your soul?
That you have not turned over to God for Him to control.

Perhaps with all your heart you try and try again,
But failure is often when you are defeated by sin.
You might see yourself worthless for God's service to fulfill,
And it's difficult to see a way back when you're out of God's Will.

But everyone has their setbacks please understand.
The best of faithful Christians fall short of life's demands.
So we must ask for God's forgiveness, as we humbly pray,
He is will forgive us, if from the sin we turn away.

For the bible says "Little Children, see that you sin not".
But if we fail to remember this, God's Love forgets us not.
For Jesus is our advocate to our Father on High,
And we are covered by His blood, until our Redemption draws nigh.

Therefore the distance you've strayed cannot leave His eyes above.
So do not think it is too late to return to His Holy Love.

It's Never Too Late for Love

Life is a wonder with all its many things,
Sometimes I am amazed by what a day will bring.

Yet there are many things, in my life I can't explain,
Like the pathway of a river, or the falling of the rain.

Or how beautiful a flower, never fails to bloom,
Awaiting spring's arrival, after a winter's doom.

Oceans that stretch for miles and miles, seem to meet the sky,
Mountains that never shake or fall in perfect pose stand high.

Many questions I cannot answer, I must say honestly,
But I know one day it will be revealed to me.

For God is in control of life; His presence is so great,
And all things are in His time, as He is never late.

And so it is with my tender heart that I will give away,
When God allows for me to meet, my chosen love one day.

This will make my single life, a special life for two,
Serving God in everything, in all we say and do.

But even if I grow old, without a marriage vow,
I know if I'm walking with the Lord, I will be fine somehow.

For everything is in God's time on earth and Heaven above,
So please believe me when I say, it's never too late for love.

Lesson of Love

I waited impatiently for God to provide someone in my life,
But He revealed it was not in His time, and so I carried strife.
Feeling bitter and angry, I searched to find my love,
Not wanting any help from God, or any from above.

Even though I knew God held my future in the palm of His Hand,
I still turned my back on Him, refusing to understand.
I decided I was going to find someone of my very own,
For I was not going to spend my life living all alone.

I soon found many loves; some were good and bad,
But it never was enough and I was very sad.
I had people all around me, and I was not alone anymore,
But I had a homesick feeling for what I had before.

For I knew I was headed for trouble since I was not in God's Will,
And the fantasy I had been chasing was never going to be real.
So I realized the only solution in finding a love so true,
Was to return to my Savior who's Love I first knew.

Look Up! "Broken-Hearts"

Many eyes are filled with tears, and have suffered broken hearts.
Many lives have ruptured, when all their dreams fell apart.
And at one time or another, we all have felt the pain,
When someone thought carelessly and left us in the rain.

Someone who we loved, suddenly said "goodbye",
And now we feel completely alone, as we question why?
But there are no answers or reasons, for such a cruel betray,
Just an empty feeling, with nothing left to say.

And though our heart still cries out for, the love we thought was true,
We now must try to start over, and find someone that's new.
So let us look up! "Broken hearts", someone is standing by,
For Jesus wants to wipe away, every tear we cry.

He wants to replace our past loves, with His Love so pure,
And heal the hurt and deepened scars, with His Everlasting Cure.
And He will pick up the pieces that have been shattered in our soul,
If we give Him our Love, and complete control.

If we let Jesus mend our broken hearts, then no one can destroy,
The special heart, filled with His Love, and His Endless Joy.

Mercy

I wanted to ski a certain trail without a single mistake,
Something I had to prove to myself for my own sake.

The first time I fell a lot in front of all my friends.
As they waited patiently until we reached the end.

The second time that I skied the trail; I seemed to do okay,
But I still fell and showed fear along the way.

Finally I decided to ski this trail alone,
Trusting God all the way I started out on my own.

This time I skied the trail perfectly without a single fall,
Knowing and believing that God controlled it all.

The trail I skied was called "Mercy" and every time I fell,
I was reminded of Gods Mercy that has saved me from Hell.

For in this life I've often failed and fallen far behind,
But the Grace of God lifts me up every single time.

He sustains my life with His Power and the Mercy of His Love,
Until the day I stand perfect with Him in Heaven above.

Romance Made in Heaven

Taking walks late at night,
Dinner for two by candlelight.
A couple watching a fire's glow,
While music plays soft and low.

Gazing at stars above or running along the beach,
Romantic moments such as these are often not in my reach.
But as I wait patiently for someone to come along,
I already know my heart has found just where it belongs.

For all the love and devotion that is felt here in my heart,
Has been claimed by my Lord, each and every part.
For I first must give my life to God, before I am able to find,
Someone here upon the earth to share with them what's mine.

And all the walks at nightfall would not matter much,
If I were to live a life without my Master's Touch.
For all the stars in the sky would not be much to see,
If I didn't first know the One who created them for me.

And my relationship with Jesus is the best I've ever known,
For I never have to worry about being at home alone.
For I have a Romance made in Heaven with fellowship so sweet,
And just knowing that my Lord loves me, makes my life complete.

Sacrificing Comfort, Accepting Change

Finding friendship, discovering love,
Feelings of encouragement, blessings from above.
Living life to its fullest, each one does their part,
But soon come the bad times which trouble the heart.

Confusion, pain, bitter feelings of doubt,
Lead us in depression, not wanting to come out.
Perhaps a heart has been broken or a life has been re-arranged,
But situations sometimes force us to accept change.

We don't like it and we rebel even though it may be for our best,
But often these changes put our faith to the test.
We must be strong enough to leave our comfort zone,
In order to face dangers of the unknown.

As Christians we do not have to fear the trials that we will face,
Because it's in these changing times that we grow in God's Grace.
So let us sacrifice any comfort that keeps us from God's Plan,
And may the changes of our future be directed by God's Hand.

That Special Someone

I often would awake each morning, with an eagerness to find,
Someone just for me, someone so kind.

I would search the whole day through, only to find despair,
Of finding that "Special Someone" was not anywhere.

Then discouraged I would be, alone once more,
And I would go home, lonely as before.

Depressed and afraid not wanting to be alone,
I finally cried out to God, for someone of my own.

I told Him I was tired and filled with so much doubt,
Of looking for that someone, I could not live without.

I knew I had prayed before and wept bitter tears,
But living my life alone was my greatest fear.

For even though "Singles" are everywhere around,
I had still rather marry and try to settle down.

But in my selfishness, I didn't realize,
That my Special Someone was right before my eyes.

Someone to take care of me, Someone for me to love,
Someone in which God had sent, from above.

For that Special Someone, was sent just for me,
And He died upon a cross, to set my spirit free.

And now that I've accepted Him, my life to Him is due,
For I've found that Special Someone, that knows I'm special too!

The Love You Can't Replace

They say… "It is better to have lost than to have never loved at all",
But sometimes I question this statement in measure to its fall.

For in those wonderful moments when I felt so high,
I was only brought back down again when I heard the words "Goodbye".

My heart has been broken so many times.
And often those memories are hard to leave behind.

But there has been One Love that will never bring me down,
And that's the Love of Jesus Christ, the Perfect Love I've found.

For when I fell in Love with Him so very long ago,
I have never been happier because He loves me so.

And it is great to know that when others break my heart,
I can always rely on Him to heal the injured part.

So when I'm hurting really bad, I focus upon His face,
And it is there I always find the Love I can't replace.

The Wall

This broken heart stabs me with pain,
And I never want to love again,
I think I will build a wall.

It will keep people from hurting me,
And I can be alone for eternity,
It will stand ten feet tall.

It will guard my heart so it can't break,
And I won't feel the cruel intake,
Of someone treating me so wrong.

I won't let anyone by,
This wall will be very high,
It will always remain very strong.

This wall cannot be knocked down,
By anything or one around,
And I will not attempt to get out.

I'm not getting hurt anymore,
Things won't be as they were before,
From now on this wall is what my life's about.

These words would always be a start,
To try to hide my fragile heart,
But I never had the strength to build the wall.

Oh, I would often always try,
But I had to give up and calmly sigh,
Because I knew that it would one day fall.

For in my heart is God's sweet joy,
That I know deep down can't be destroyed,
And even if I were to succeed my goal.

His Love could still find a way,
To break through the wall someday,
For He holds the key to the bottom of my soul.

You Knew Me Lord

Every time that I would fail, is the time You would be there,
Every time that I would cry, I could feel Your loving care.

Before You had made, this beautiful earth,
You thought my life, would be of worth.

And in finding out, what I never knew,
I humbly surrendered my life to You.

Now as I look back,
I begin to see,
Before I could fall,
Your hand was stretched out for me.

With Your Love, in which to cope,
I saw in You, the Blessed Hope.

And Your Life, that You would lose,
Was lost so, I might know You.

Scripture References for Selected Poems
Chapter 2
THE HEART MENDER

The Heart Mender	Psalm 34:18
Astray	Psalm Chapter 6
Beautiful Lullaby	Zephaniah 3:17
Blessing Before Bitterness	Ephesians 4:31-32
Forgiveness of His Own	I John 2: 1-3
You Knew Me Lord	Ephesians 1: 4-5

The Trusting Time

Oh, the depth of the riches of the wisdom and knowledge of God!

How unsearchable his judgments, and his paths beyond tracing out!

"Who has known the mind of the Lord? Or who has been his counselor?"

"Who has ever given to God, that God should repay them?"

For from him and through him and for him are all things.

To him be the glory forever! Amen.

Romans 11: 33-36

CHAPTER THREE

EXPRESSIONS

Expressions

Oh my Jesus oh my soul, such blessed assurance, when You're in control,
My heart of singing, my soul of joy, no human tampering can destroy.
The plan unfolding, the purpose sure, the understanding so rich and pure,
The thought that one would interfere, Oh say it not be me I fear.

My heart expresses Your love for me, a specific journey and path to be,
I know it wisely, I know it well, Your Word of Truth to all I tell.
So run Your Delight within my being, let my song to You be singing,
Ever present Adonai, to YOU my heart, does lift this cry.

Thank you, thank you for the cross, thank you for the greatest cost!
Your Shining Glory Immanuel, came down, came fast and exploded Hell's …
Mission of destruction, the sinner's scope, because of You there is still Hope.

The cross made a way, Your blood was spilled, Your dying body made the earth stand still,
Now an empty tomb invites us all, who will follow YOU and hear Your call.

Acknowledging His Holiness

Thou Lord, You are so great and I am so small,
Though You came to earth humble, You are Holiest of all.

When I think of how Holy You are, I realize just who I am,
For I'm so unclean with sin, unto the Worthy Lamb.

My corrupt body of disgrace, leaves me with nowhere to run,
When Thy illuminating Light shines upon me, and reveals how I'm undone.

For since I live on this earth with sin and so I must be purged clean,
Before I can face my Lord and Holy King.

So create in me a clean heart Lord, and show me what to do,
For Father, I know that one day, I want to be like You.

Heaven Presents "Jesus"

Ladies and Gentlemen, you are about to behold,
Life's greatest event, to ever unfold.

For behold you now, is about to take place,
A moment that shall be filled, with Glory and Grace.

So now, without further ado, let us all sing,
As Heaven presents "JESUS", our King.

And here He is now, forever He shall reign,
Oh worthy is the Lamb, for sinners He was slain.

But now He's come to rule, in Majesty and Power,
See Him now in His Glory, as we worship Him this hour.

Such Light and Radiance, beams from His head,
As He establishes to everyone, that He is not dead!

The view of Him is astounding, as He approaches the crowd,
Heavenly Host are singing, and Praising Him aloud.

They sing "Hosanna to our King", as they fall to their knees,
For He comes to bring us joy, and everlasting peace.

And now all eyes are upon Him, as He begins to speak,
"My Children the battle is over, now you shall live with me".

Honest Worship

God, I want to worship You more!
I want my tears my heart ...
To pour out worship for only YOU!

For You are my Christ, You are my King,
My Savior who gives my heart, a reason to sing,
Creator, over every living thing!

My honest worship and sacrifice do I bring.
Underneath Your Guiding Wings,
Let nothing far or in between,
Ever stop me from entering...

Into Your Holy Presence.

My Constant

Where can I go, that you are not there?
For my Lord, you are everywhere.
Your hand does guide me and takes me through,
The daily grind of life's issues.

The surprises and joys that I celebrate,
I receive Your blessings, when I do wait,
For Your perfect timing, to be in my life,
Your wisdom does keep me, away from much strife.

You know me and search me in the deepest part,
For You created me from Your very heart.
When I was in my mother's womb,
Even there, Your love bloomed.

Your mind is full of sovereignty,
To understand You, is too much for me.
If I find myself flying, through the sky,
Your Presence is still nearby.

On the ground, when I'm running from fear,
I can be assured that you are here.
When I choose life's hell, by my will,
It is there you are with me, leading me still.

So fill me, consume me and convict my soul,
I want to hold nothing back, from Your control,
Do not let sin break, my fellowship with You,
Restore me and dwell in my spirit anew.

Let the dark not cover me, without seeing a shine,
Of Your Radiant Presence, in my life intertwined.
With Your Glory, Honor and Power to show,
Your Holiness and Majesty in my life overflowed.

Poured Out

Tears of Brokenness and strength,
Poured right out of me,
Your Truth to hear aloud,
It did my heart so proud.

Yet, the thought of just one soul,
Not knowing the death toll,
Made my heart just break,
And my body did shake.

Father, I must not hesitate,
Before it is too late,
Burden my heart to tell,
So others won't go to Hell.

Prepare Me for Eternity

Though I've never seen Your face,
I've felt Your Saving Grace.

I worship You day by day,
Trying to follow in Your Way.

But sometimes I wonder,
And my heart often ponders,
If I really know, who You are to me...

For Thou Art Holy and so great,
And You know my destined fate.

Though You are a King of Power,
You watch over me every hour.

As You live in Heaven above,
Reaching out to me with Love,
I'm surrounded by You, in all I see...

But Lord I want to know You more,
For Thou Art the One I adore.

So fill my human empty soul,
And in my life take full control.

Not leaving one part for my gain,
But always confirming that You shall reign,
As You prepare me for Eternity.

Quiet Time with God

Walking by a seaside,
Distant down the shore,
Listening to the waves,
The tide rolls in once more.

Visions, in my mind,
As I imagine all of this,
Running from my troubles,
Going back for what I missed.

Knowing that God,
Knows every part of me,
While I enjoy HIS quiet time,
That will last for an eternity...

The Great Ecstasy

As I watch the clouds, swiftly pass in the sky,
I hear songs from the birds, as over me they fly.
While enjoying this moment, I begin to slip away,
Releasing my problems, and all I've been through today.

I imagine the rapture, where in the air I will rise,
To meet my coming King, and Lord most High.
For I can't wait until, He scatters the night,
Filling every corner, of this earth, with His Light.

Such majesty my eyes, will one day behold,
His coming will be GREAT, as prophets have foretold.
Because I will see Jesus, in all His Glory as He is,
And all Praise and Honor will forever be His.

And I look forward in hearing, His words so sweet,
"Well done my faithful servant, Come sit at my feet".

Timing the Waves

Oceans of splendor... the bluest of blue,
Always help me ... feel closer to you.

The waves crashing... with such loud sound,
Remind me of Your Power ... which is all around.

The seagulls that scamper ... along the shore,
Are so much like me ... for I am not much more...

Always timing Your waves ...with my selfish will,
Trusting in my own way ... I get wetter still.

So, if I will time Your waves ... by Thine own design,
Then I shall walk on water ... and the Blessing will be mine.

Victorious Over All

One day I'll join an army, where I will take a stand,
Along with other Christians, for our Lord's command.

Together we will fight, for truth and inner peace,
And vengeance will be God's, when His wrath shall be released.

We will be fighting against evil, and God's Love will prevail,
When Satan and his angels, are cast into Hell.

Then the Victory, will be the Lord's, as we shout and sing,
Praise be to our God, and our Heavenly King.

But until then we fight a battle, in our lives every day,
Against the powers of darkness, that try to stand in our way.

Yet, God gives us courage, so we can fight back.
Through trials and temptations, that can get us off track,

And with the Sword of Truth, to guide us, we will remain strong,
We can defeat the enemy, and all that is wrong.

We may not win every battle, sometimes we will fall,
But we will keep hope in knowing, God is VICTORIOUS OVER ALL.

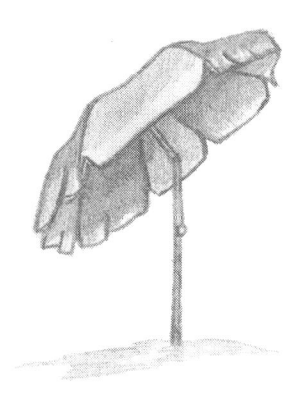

Scripture References for Selected Poems
Chapter 3
EXPRESSIONS

Expressions	Romans 11: 33-36
Acknowledging His Holiness	Isaiah Chapter 6
Heaven Presents Jesus	Revelation 1: 7-8
My Constant	Psalm Chapter 139
Prepare Me for Eternity	I Corinthians 2: 9-12
Quiet Time with God	Psalm 42: 7-8
The Great Ecstasy	I Thessalonians 4: 14-18
Timing the Waves	Psalm 107: 28-30
Victorious Over All	Ephesians 6: 10-18

"Again, truly I tell you that if two of you on earth agree about anything they ask for, it will be done for them by my Father in heaven. For where two or three gather in my name, there am I with them."

Matthew 18: 19-20

CHAPTER FOUR

THE POWER OF PRAYER

The Power of Prayer

Often we've heard the phrase, "All we can do now is pray",
When the misfortunes of life, seem to fall our way.

We seem to say it without knowing its fullness of power,
Not having enough hope, to brighten our dark hour.

Oh, we can feel God with us, and we know that He cares,
But we wish we could do more, than just go to Him in prayer.

But let us take a moment, away from our fear,
To see what we are missing, that is so very dear.

Our prayer to God, is a miracle in itself,
And we shouldn't take it lightly, nor set it on a shelf.

We have a direct communication, which shouldn't be ignored,
It gives us access to God, through Jesus Christ our Lord.

And with this special blessing, we can do so much,
As God hears our prayers, many lives can be touched.

A Christian's Prayer

Dear Lord, I thank-you for saving me,
Out of my trouble and misery,
Help me to do exactly what You say,
And stay close beside me every day.

When I fail to understand,
Let me see Your guiding hand,
If my friends find fault with You,
Give me the knowledge to know what to do.

Help me to love my enemies as well as my friends,
And keep me away from wrong, Amen.

A Prayer for Grief

One night as I knelt by my bed,
I prayed, as I bowed my head,
In despair to the Lord I cried,
Dear Lord, I am so terrified!
And here I sit alone, so sad,
Only looking at what I had.

Trying to think how I will ever cope,
For I've lost all happiness and I fear all hope.
So give me courage and the strength to go on,
And help me, through You, to remain strong.
For I don't know what I will do,
So I'll leave it in your hands, and I give it to You.
As I raised myself from the floor,
I heard the Lord speak, like never before...

MY DEAR CHILD, YOU ARE MINE, AND ALWAYS WILL BE,
AND YOU CAN BE STRONG IF YOU LEAN UPON ME.
FOR MY LOVE WILL CARRY YOU THROUGH,
AND YOU NEED NOT FEAR WHAT YOU WILL DO.
NOW JUST REST AND HAVE FAITH IN ME THIS HOUR,
TRUST IN ME AND MY HOLY POWER.
I WILL WATCH OVER YOU WITH MY CARE,
SO YOU NEED NOT FEAR, BECAUSE I AM HERE.

A Single's Prayer

Lord, I've heard the old saying, "You can't hurry love" many times before,
And though it would be nice to settle down, I know there's so much more.

Like serving You, and others who are in need,
As I follow You daily wherever You may lead.

And on the days when I'm not happy and the confidence is not there,
Help me to be content and satisfied, by lifting You up in prayer.

And when I'm staying at home while my friends are out on dates,
Grant me with the patience so upon You I will wait.

For I want to feel Your Peace Dear Lord, abolishing all fear,
As You re-assure my lonely heart that You are standing near.

Seeking You first with trust and love is where I must begin,
To find a happy restful heart, loving You more and more, Amen.

My Prayer of Praise

Dear Lord, this prayer is just for You,
Though my small words, will never do.
For they cannot begin to show,
The greatest things, I've come to know.

And these words cannot say,
All that is on my heart today.
In times of my life, I can look back and see,
How very close, You walked with me.

And when I would trust You, with all my fears,
You were there, through all those years.
And now my faith in You has grown,
No greater Love, I've ever known.

So, in Your name, this honor be given,
The Highest Praise, throughout the heavens.
For You are worthy, my Lord Most High,
For my sins, You chose to die.

But in the tomb, one could not hold,
Such power and love that would unfold.
And my life to You I gave,
So my soul, You would save.

So if anything, I ever do,
Does not give the Glory to You,
Let me count it all loss and strive to gain,
The things for You that will remain.

Prayers Down the Hall

There's a light from a bedroom, I can see down the hall,
As I make my way to it, I hear my mother's call.

She's praying ever softly, as tears roll down her face,
Words even sweeter than Amazing Grace.

And Jesus and the angels, are gathering around,
They hear my mother praying, as she kneels to the ground.

And I have never heard, a more precious sound,
Than to hear my mother praying, as she kneels there, in her gown.

Prayer for a Friend

Dear Lord , Please encourage my friend,
She is feeling very blue.

Let my friend feel the Radiant Joy,
That comes from only You.

Reach down and touch her hurting heart,
With Your healing from above.

Giving her the strength that she needs
To help the ones she loves.

And she and I will praise You Lord,
As on Your name we call.

Because we know You love us so,
And You watch over all.

Prayer for Contentment

Lord, I am thankful for all that You have done for me,
And in Your sovereign mind ... all You do see,

You own it all Lord ... it is Yours to take away,
I pray You would be satisfied upon that tested day.

I pray that I am found faithful, even with life's demands,
And I would still be thankful, even with empty hands.

If I do not have eyes to see what is all around,
If I lose the ability to hear the many sounds,

If I do not have food to eat and not a place to sleep.
If I have nothing material, this reminder let me keep...

Your Name is Exalted Lord, in times of misery and pain.
You create the sunshine but You also send the rain,

Your Perfect Love, Eternal Life and Hope to Light my way,
Provides me with everything, I'll ever need today.

So let this prayer of contentment be the offering I bring,
Because, until all I need is found in You ... I do not have a thing.

Prayer for Faith

Dear Lord, encourage me to have faith that can move a mountain.
Faith that will stand the test of time, faith that will cease to let You down,
Or follow far behind...

Faith, in which to believe, without evidence of proof,
You are God Alone, the One who stands for truth.
Faith in which to follow You, while others turn away,
Faith in which to make it through, on less brighter days.

Faith that I may have in You, when doubting comes around,
Faith in finding and reaching for those higher planes of ground.
For even as a Christian my faith is sometimes small,
And when the world threatens me, I have no faith at all!

Grant me faith with confidence, in all You expect me to be,
Faith that shows a reflection of You inside of me.
I pray this prayer with all my heart, that whatsoever I do,
That all Thy Glory and all my faith holds forever fast in You.

Prayer of Forgiveness

I lost my temper again today, just as I've done before,
Things didn't go my way, and I questioned You once more.

I know You've told me that if I have faith, You will see me through,
But even when I try so hard, I'm forever failing You.

But You are there in all my pain, to see my every tear,
Reassuring my bewildered soul, that You are standing near.

For when I take my eyes off You, I put fear in Your place,
Completely losing focus, upon Your precious face.

So, Father forgive me of my selfish ways, and all my many sins,
And let me learn to trust You more, by putting You first again.

Prayer Time

In the early morning hour
In the afternoon or mid-day,
When the sun has gone down,
Is when I often pray.

I pray for all my family,
My friends and those I know.
I pray for God to guide us,
To the places we may go.

I said a prayer for you,
For God to bless your heart,
To show you what to do,
For a fresh new start.

Each and every day,
He will give you grace
Leading you along,
In whatever you may face.

So if you feel discouraged,
If you feel despair,
Remember to take courage,
He is always there.

Seminary Student's Prayer

Dear Lord, I love You, You are so gracious to me,
For giving me the opportunity...

To serve You through school, and learn more about Your Word,
And to share with others all that I've heard.

But I sometimes fail to understand,
To see what You have for me in Your Plan.

And even though I'm serving You,
I feel I might not make it through...

The tests are hard and the studying is long,
It gets rough, while traveling on...

My financial means are kind of down,
And I miss my family in my home town.

I know I cry and complain a lot too,
Please help me, in knowing what I'm to do...

Remind me again that You are in control,
And ease my mind and calm my soul.

The Unanswered Prayer

When times are bad, we turn to prayer,
In faith that God, will meet us there.

And as we kneel upon bended knee,
Earnestly, God hears our plea.

There are times, we pray with care,
When it seems our hearts, reach despair…

We pray so long, with many tears,
And think our prayers, God does not hear.

But He hears all prayers, despite the size,
And we must always, realize…

That He always, answers every cry,
And He will never, pass us by.

You see He answers prayers, within His time,
And we cannot afford, to leave behind…

Anything that we must share,
That should be taken, to God in prayer.

God answers all prayers, this I know,
Sometimes with a yes, sometimes with a no.

And sometimes the answer He gives is to wait,
But in answering our prayers He is never late.

So, do not think that God does not care,
For there is no such thing as an unanswered prayer.

Scripture References for Selected Poems
Chapter 4
THE POWER OF PRAYER

The Power of Prayer	Matthew 18: 19-20
A Prayer for Grief	Psalm 119:76
My Prayer of Praise	Philippians 3: 7-9
Prayer for Contentment	Hebrews 13:2
Prayer for Faith	Mark 11: 20-24
Prayer of Forgiveness	Psalm Chapter 51
Seminary Student's Prayer	Philippians 1:6
The Unanswered Prayer	Matthew 7: 7-8

You will go out in joy and be led forth in peace;

the mountains and hills will burst into song before you,

and all the trees of the field will clap their hands.

Isaiah 55:12

CHAPTER FIVE

VIEW FROM THE TOP

View From the Top

Standing on the mountain, gazing all around,

So high above everything, where there is no sound.

No birds are singing, the wind is blowing slow,

Not a soul is around; just me... my God and snow.

Admiring God's Creation, in beautiful array,

Feeling His Mighty Presence... I bow my head to pray.

God's Spirit whispers to me, His Loving words of care,

That I am not alone, for He is EVERYWHERE!

A Hope for Spring

Many nights I have felt an icy pain of despair,
The sun's daylight hid within the frosty air.
Yet now I feel the joy unfolding,
As winter loses the grip it was holding.

Safely it arrives once more,
Spring enters through winter's door.
And I see the sun peering through,
As if to say, "God still loves you".

It touches leaves upon the trees,
The flowers bloom in delicacy.
Reminders of God's Loving Care,
Erase life's winter that was hard to bear.

Soon, even troubles will pass,
They cannot stand they will not last.
For the cold and gloom must depart,
As now the Hope of Spring grows in my heart.

A Joy for Summer

As the sun beats down, I scamper to my fun,
Into the folly of my neglect before the day is done.

I haven't a care in the world; I leave my thoughts of You,
And I rush into my own defeat with selfish attitude.

Soon the temptations lead me away, where willingly I go,
Fooled by alluring voices in which I do not know.

The happiness that I once had, from the very start,
Has broken my spirit and heavy is my heart.

Yet, it's in the sadness of my soul, I remember vividly,
How it was when I walked with You and You walked with me.

So, in my distress I cry out Your Holy name,
To ask You to forgive me, of all of my sin and shame.

My love for You is now renewed; my joy in You is restored,
Oh Lord I will worship You and praise You as before.

A Peace for Fall

Leaves of red and gold, gently they are falling,
A gentle season is now here, little birds are calling.

Autumn has arrived; it's time to unwind,
And take a moment out and spend some time,

Reflecting upon Your Mercies and Faithfulness to me,
Walking every step with You in quiet company.

And if I focus upon Your Holiness and Majesty so true,
My heart will be satisfied with Real Peace, that only comes from You.

Even the Trees Bow

The birds sing His Praises, with melodies of song,
The wind blows His Spirit, which carries on and on.

The rain sends showers of blessing, for His delight,
While thunder rumbles a bolder praise, throughout the darkest night.

Lightning flashes in the sky, displaying gratitude for His Power,
Everything gives Praise to God, in His Holy hour.

The flowers grow with bright color, for His Glory and His Grace,
In fields of the greenest grass, covering every space.

For He deserves the Highest Praise, that this earth can boast,
Especially from the human man, for God loves us the most.

For even the trees bow in the wind, giving Honor unto the King,
And so should God receive Great Praise, from every living thing.

Faith for Winter

Lonely, depressed and blue, the snow falls to the ground,
Cold, wet, and dreary is the weather all around.

My heart is distilled, longing after more,
Hidden is the Faith I had long before…

Now the winter comes, with her whispering wind,
And I am troubled with trials, in my life again.

So, now I call to You, to rescue me from despair,
Spark my Faith once more and kindle it with care.

Cover me my Lord, against the cold of winter,
And I will lean on You, as Your Presence I do enter.

Safe from all that can harm me, safe from every fear,
I will build my life around You, for You are always near.

God's Creation

As the sun rises, with its morning of duty,
It awakens the wild, with its wonder and beauty.

There was a storm the night before,
But now it is gone, the rains are no more.

Tears from the rain kissed the leaves of the trees,
And in the air you can feel, a soft summer breeze.

The birds are now starting to fly and to sing,
Beautiful songs for the new day of spring.

There's a stream nearby, such a beautiful sight,
As it flows by, the water catches the light.

The deer gather round it, so timid and shy,
And as they do, a frog goes hopping by.

A wonderful place to get away from it all,
In winter, spring, summer or fall.

It is a beautiful place, God's Creation for me,
And it fills me with peace and serenity.

His Unchanging Love

The cold wind is blowing, as the trees begin to sway,
A part of nature's life, starts withering away.

Snow now is falling, upon the wilted grass,
Proving to everyone that winter is here at last.

But soon a sign of Spring will sprout up from the ground,
Bringing forth rejuvenation, to all that is around.

A celebration will be given, in honor of new birth,
To announce the fresh new start, now growing on the earth.

And as the flowers blossom, coloring every space,
The days start getting warmer, as Summer takes her place.

But jus as soon as nature welcomes her, like a long lost friend,
The time of fun and play, also have to end.

For green leaves start to change, into colors of red and gold,
And so the final season of Autumn, begins to unfold.

The changing seasons remind us, of how things must be,
In life's everyday situations, that involves you and me.

Just like many good times, that we all have known,
They must say goodbye again, leaving us alone.

And the bad times that seem to threaten us, filling us with fear,
Will in a moment quickly pass, and start to disappear.

But we can be reassured, and our faith shall sustain,
The joy of knowing God's Love will always remain.

For He is here by our sides, from the Winter to the Fall,
Providing shelter for all who come, in answer to His call.

So watch not the Seasons that pass, but focus your eyes above,
On God's consistent Saving Grace, and His Unchanging Love.

Many Glimpses of God's Glory

We can feel God's touch in the wind; see His beauty in each flower,
We hear His silence, in ocean sounds, as He's with us each waking hour.

So many times we've seen Him, though it's not been visually,
For His Spirit is all around us, many glimpses of God's Glory.

No one has ever seen God's face, or has been embraced in His arms,
Yet we know that He is here, protecting us from harm.

Yes, many glimpses of God's Glory, have been seen throughout time,
And they still exist today, for those who want to find...

More than lovely words, or a feeling from above,
But by one who will step out in faith, and accept His Love.

Because in the glimpses of God's Glory, we can all share a part,
With His Glorious Son Jesus Christ, if He lives inside our hearts.

Seeds of Encouragement

Plant a seed of KINDNESS and watch with sweet surprise...
The happiness of others and joy within their eyes.

Plant a seed of PRAYER and be amazed to hear...
The answers from a Loving God, for those whom you hold dear.

Plant a seed of LOVE and reach out to someone new...
The time given to many will return back to you.

Plant a seed of HOPE to everyone you know...
and you will be ENCOURAGED how all the seeds will GROW!

Spiritual Sight

God gave me my eyes, that I might see,
The sun that shines, so bright on me.

Mountains, of majesty, that reach so high,
And rainbows, of promise, that color the sky.

I thank Him for all the things I have seen,
I have found pleasure, in everything.

For only His Love, has opened my eyes,
To behold the beauty, which around me lies.

And if I should find my sight taken away,
Only left seeing shadows, of colorless grey.

He is my Lord and He leads the way,
So I will follow Him and continue to pray.

I shall not stumble in the dark a fright,
For God has given me spiritual sight.

Storms of Life

Last night the storms that beat my window sill,
And had thundered all around,
Were the same storms that beat the weeds,
Yet sprung flowers from the ground?

The lightening that brightened the night,
And struck in the sky,
Also re-assured my faith,
That God was close by.

The rain that fell for hours,
That I felt lasted so long,
Provided drinks for little birds,
That would sing His morning song.

So I got down beside my bed,
And I fell down on my knees,
In prayer I praised Him for the rain,
And for His inner peace...

For that is when I realized...

It's in the storms of life, when we should come to know,
That God is only watering us, for His sunshine,
That will someday help us GROW!

The Sunshine

The rain that we've been blessed with,
Has left us for a while,

As the warm sun comes peeking out,
To show its bright new smile.

It makes me feel all good inside,
As depression leaves my soul.

And my heart is glad once more,
As happiness takes control.

For when I enjoy the sunshine,
And all its pleasantry,

I'm constantly reminded of,
God's Special Love for me.

Scripture References for Selected Poems
Chapter 5
VIEW FROM THE TOP

View From the Top	Isaiah 55:12
Even the Trees Bow	Psalm Chapter 148
His Unchanging Love	Psalm 89: 1-2
Many Glimpses of God's Glory	Ephesians 1: 17-23
Storms of Life	Psalm 147:8

The LORD is my strength and my shield; my heart trusts in him, and he helps me. My heart leaps for joy, and with my song I praise him.

Psalm 28:7

CHAPTER SIX
THE TRUSTING TIME

The Trusting Time

Storms are over me the clouds are so gray,
And yet this is not what casts my fear.
Tis the sunny time when all is at play,
The daily grind that I live each year.

Moments of bliss seem fleeting,
Discouragement takes me unaware,
The enemy gleefully depleting,
The Hand of God's Infinite Care.

Why does my heart who knows Jesus,
Struggle with insecurities beyond measure.
Why must my mind put up such a fuss,
When it holds such an eternal treasure.

Sometimes verses are read and songs are sung,
Yet, the Presence of God is quiet still.
The enemy gloats and has his fun,
But, Lord, this is not THY WILL ...

No, this is the only the Trusting Time,
Oh that my heart would pass thy test...
And a stronger Faith in you I'd find,
While I abide within Your chest.

A Valentine of Praise

Once I held hands with my love so true,
While walking in a park and sitting in a pew.
But now I lift my hands to You,
Use me Lord in all I do.

Once I spoke with romantic gestures,
To my mate and sweetest treasure.
But now I will offer in highest measure,
My voice in praise to bring You pleasure.

Yet, when many memories in my mind repeat,
My life sometimes seems incomplete…
But with my tears so bittersweet,
Let me anoint Thy precious feet.

For though my mate has passed away,
And others know not what to say,
With prayers of hope I humbly pray,
So help me live for You each day.

Angels Are Here

Angels are here,
They hover, they are silent,
Yet they are very near.
Quietly in the midst,
They listen to every prayer.

Through the dark shadows,
On the brightest day,
They watch they linger...
And hear us when we pray.

Protecting us, surrounding us
They are angels unaware,
They are invisible reminders,
That God still cares.

In times of weeping,
In times of joy,
There constant presence...
Evil can't destroy.

God's angels of light,
Showing us His way,
Standing right beside us,
As they guard us this day.

As We Stand

As we all stand together, in a humble way,
Of what we all remember, on that certain day...

When death had stolen the joy, and nailed it to a cross,
Of which our souls ponder every moment, of how great the cost.

But we can stand in Hope, because of that Glorious Hour...
Because Jesus Resurrected, with Great Majesty and Power.

So now our hearts extend, so others too may see,
God's Love demonstrated, through our unity.

For we stand in Victory, unto all that remains,
As we give Everlasting Glory, to our Lord who REIGNS.

Fear and Fret Not

It seems today's research and medical reports,
Have negative findings which their statistics supports.
Health care wars escalate with no resolution,
The ozone is heavy because of pollution.

Children can no longer be safe at our schools,
Because selfish bullies are making the rules.
There are new health warnings on the labels we see,
Bringing with them fear of cancers or obesity.

And the medicines we have at home on our shelf,
Can cause side effects that may worsen our health.
There are growing concerns for all the foods that we eat,
From fruits and vegetables to tainted meat.

Many perilous floods, fires and destructive storms,
Have struck everywhere to bring great harm.
There is fear of layoffs and mortgage collapse…
There is fret of catastrophe to our polar caps.

The global warming is always getting worse,
While others fear asteroids may fall on the earth.
There is much on the news today
That brings doom and great dismay…

Of disease, famine and pestilence,
It can scare anyone and shake confidence.
There are viruses we can catch every time we sneeze,
And who can forget those killer bees!

The Trusting Time

There is so much bad news surrounding us,
And it does seem logical to make a fuss...
Over the failing economy and debt
And all that hasn't happened yet?

It's true the situation appears to be grim
And the thought of a bright future looks very dim.
Yet... encouraging scriptures are there for us to find,
For each troubled heart and fearful mind.

You see, Jesus prophesied many years ago,
That one day these things would be so.
So really, we shouldn't be surprised,
That these tribulations are before our eyes,

Because we live in a world that is fallen,
And creation is groaning for what Satan has stolen.
We must be patient to watch, wait and learn,
As each day grows closer to our Lord's return.

God alone is the giver and taker of life,
No matter the circumstance or level of strife.
He is in control and does give the command,
For each trial and blessing that comes from His hand.

So that we might grow and bear fruit,
With God's direction of a Holy Pursuit.
Jesus Himself is our Promise of Peace,
Through His Word we will find release.

Yes, Jesus wants to set us free,
So all our fears and frets will cease.

Fear of Heights

I wanted to go to the top,
But my fear of heights caused me to stop...

As I watched everyone get in a ski chair,
Quickly they flew up in the air.

Until all my friends had left me behind,
And I was standing alone at the end of the line.

I took a deep breath and held on tight,
Trying to hide my fear of heights.

All at once, I felt totally free,
As I admired all of the scenery.

So we must have faith in all we do,
That God will always see us through.

You see, sometimes our faith is weak,
When we must fly to mountain peaks.

But God will not let us fall,
When He cares and loves us all.

God's Plan

I awoke each morning, with the early dawn,
I would get ready for work, and go merrily along.

I would forget to see things from a Christian view,
As I just kept pushing myself and struggling through.

Oh, I love God, with all my heart,
But sometimes I was too busy to do my part.

Yes, I went to church every Sunday to pray,
And I was thankful to the Lord each day.

Still I would work so hard and it was difficult to find,
A few moments with God for a quiet time.

I would complain to Him when things went wrong,
Until the whole perspective of His Plan would be gone.

You see, all at once I realized,
God was not who I idolized.

I loved Him sure, but I couldn't see,
How precious His Presence was to me.

My life was filled with so much strife,
Since God wasn't first in my life.

So, I asked forgiveness of my selfish ways,
And I started reading my bible every day.

Now the moments are sweeter because I understand,
Fellowship with Him is part of God's Plan.

God's Way

As I admire the beauty of the earth, that God has created for me,
I'm constantly reminded of His Love, by everything I see.
And though times of discouragement, sometimes make me feel blue,
I know my God is faithful, and He will see me through.

So I try to see things God's Way, using my spiritual sight,
While following the right path, which is directed by His Light.
I listen with my heart, to what He has to say,
To His words of wisdom, for He is the Way.

So I'm leaning not on my own understanding, or what I think is best,
But I'm trusting completely in God, through every trial and test.
For my ways are not His Ways, and it is clear to me,
Just who holds my future, and who knows my destiny.

Grief (The Mysterious Gift)

When God made people like you and me,
He gave us vision for our eyes to see,
He gave us sound for our ears to hear,
He gave us Love for our hearts to bear.

He gave us thought for our minds to know,
He gave us meaning for our lives to grow.
Yet, in the times when our soul feels despair,
From losing a loved one taken out of our care.

It's then we often ask God... Why?
With bitter tears He hears our cry.
You see He has given us special attention,
To the pain we feel that we don't often mention.
The doubts, the anger... He understands,
All is held in His Loving Hand.

He gives us tears to clear our eyes...
Beyond the storms we see blue skies.
He gives us encouragement to hear the words,
Like Hope and Strength in the songs of birds.
He gives us time to deal with strife,
The Touch of His Grace guards our life.

These gifts from God help me and you.
During moments of grief, He will carry us through.

I Cannot Feel

I cannot feel the emptiness and pain, of what you're feeling today,
And I do not have the power or strength, to remove your thoughts of dismay.

I cannot unfold the hope of tomorrow, that I know you will find again,
I can only offer you my deepest sympathy, as one of your many friends.

But my Savior who is standing by, with all His Loving Grace,
Can offer you the peace you need, for whatever you may face.

For He can restore your wounded soul, and mend your broken heart,
With all His consolation, that will make your sorrow depart.

As a Friend He will bear your burdens, and all, your heartaches share,
So I will keep you in my thoughts, and in my every prayer.

In the Clearing

The older that I get, the more I understand,
How fragile life is slipping through my hands.

The emotions that I feel, that well up in my soul,
Seem meaningless, for I am not in control.

You created my being, when I was just a thought,
I grew with your wisdom, in which I have been taught.

And now as each year passes, I can see so much,
A pathway is marked for me, with Your gentle loving touch.

As youthfulness leaves my body and lines appear on my face,
I feel Your presence even stronger, though life has left its trace.

When changes begin to happen, and seem to creep up on me,
I cherish the moments of my Faith, with childlike simplicity.

This home on earth is fleeting, oh now I see it true,
I am only in the clearing, until I live with You.

In the Suffering

Today as I awakened,
The pain would not go away…

So, I struggled to find some strength,
And face the routine day.

On most mornings it's hard to ignore…
Such pain and misery.

And though some days are bearable,
The pain is there constantly.

Still…

I will seek out a place of refuge,
A place of Peace for me…

When I meet with my Loving Savior,
In quiet company.

I will open up the pages of His Word,
And all its many treasures.

I will sing a song of Praise,
Of His love which can't be measured.

And then when He lifts me up,
His Presence will fill my soul.

Because in Him I find everything,
He is in complete control.

So today I will remember His Truth,
And the Promise that His Word brings…

For He is with me every hour,
Even in the suffering.

Just Remember

Days are often filled with uncertain turns and twists,
Some are good and bad, while others merely exist.
We try to make the best of things, to give us strength to cope,
But when tragedy seems to befall us, it takes away our hope.

Being a Christian has its moments, in which we cannot see,
A direct path where God is leading us to a victory.
When clouds of darkness and shadows of despair try to conceal our joy,
We sometimes will fall into depression, which seeks only to destroy.

But if we look beyond our situations, and just follow in God's Will,
Then our eyes are kept on Jesus, and our spirit He will fill.
And we can take comfort in knowing, that one day we will see,
The Blessed Hope of the Risen Christ, throughout eternity.

Just to Say

Seasons pass so very fast,
And it's hard to make a moment last.
But we live the best we can,
Even though we misunderstand.

Life's disappointments and unfair ways,
Can take away the brighter days.
Things are fine until there is change,
Then everything is rearranged...

But life here is temporary and we shouldn't be sad,
A Great Day is coming, when all shall be glad.
So, let in some Light and don't be sorrowed,
Our time on earth is only borrowed!

For if we have Jesus in our hearts,
One day from this world we will depart!
We'll leave this body, to which we are bound,
And fly to plains, of higher ground.

So I hope you realize that in all you do,
I care a lot and God does too!

Looking Beyond

Today my cross is heavy, in which I daily bear,
But I'm comforted by God's Spirit, which is forever there.

Today my soul is weary, and my footsteps are very weak,
But I know my God is Faithful, and His promises He will keep.

For one day when Christ returns, He shall split the sky,
And His face will be seen by every beholden eye.

Then all will sing His praises, with a joyous song,
With love for our Redeemer, in which we've waited for so long.

It's the troubles and trials we endure, that often bring us defeat,
But these crosses will one day be exchanged for crowns,
So we can lay them at Jesus feet.

Panic Attack

It takes me, controls me and holds me in captivity,
There's darkness, no freedom, no peace I feel or see...

I find it in the smallest things, like the news on the TV.
My life can spin around and round until I'm dizzy...

But Lord, you still hold me, you steady me,
In Your Love, I find hope of such serenity.

Doubt may take stolen hours and frightened I may be...
But, you are still in control and hold eternity.

My purpose is sure; my future is secure, my destiny...
Fear is now losing its grip, like calmness in a sea.

Now that I have cried out to You, down on bended knee,
I feel Your Peace once more, because You heard my plea.

Pity Party

When I looked at myself and saw a troubled me...
Trying to escape, from all my reality...
I turned to my friends, who seemed to have it all,
But not caring how I felt, they didn't hear my call.

And so I began to dream, of what could have been,
But by thinking of the past, I was sad once again.
So, I had a pity party, just me, myself and I...
And I celebrated sadness with the tears that I cried.

Heartache was there and Loneliness brought pain...
They tried to comfort me, but only caused more rain.
Then suddenly I heard a voice, beyond my silent tears,
That relieved me of my sadness and all my dreadful fears.

It was Jesus, who rescued me from my unhappy hour,
And He gave me inner strength, through His Loving Power.
He said that all my moments of sadness would erase...
If I fixed my eyes and heart upon His precious face.

So just remember friend, the next time you can't cope,
Take your eyes off yourself and see the Blessed Hope.

Point to Him

When we see someone who is broken,
Sometimes it's best, to keep our words unspoken.

If we find someone who is caught in sin,
Let us gently try to restore them again.

If someone is full of great despair,
Let them know how much you care.

If someone is ill or feeling sick,
Encouragement always does the trick.

You see even though we like to give advice and compare,
What people really need is the silence of our prayers.

Whether the person is sad, upset or distressed,
A lot of times it can be the best…

To not instruct or give information,
But rather share God's Word with exhortation.

Being very careful, that we don't control,
Or else we'll miss out on moments, that help console.

Because in every given situation no matter how grim,
God is in control and we should always point to Him.

Returning to the Valley

Oh! Leaving the mountain was sad for me,
For there I had found tranquility.

It was magical and awesome every day.
From reality it had taken me away,

I did not want to ever come down.
And go back to my own home town.

But soon I realized I had to go,
So I left behind the crystal snow.

And so I returned to the valley green,
To share with all what I had seen.

As Christians we would like to stay,
On the mountain with God each day.

Yet if we do, we will miss out,
On what life with Him, is all about.

Mountain experiences always restore,
But the valley below must not be ignored.

If we live on the mountain we cannot reach,
Those in the valley, that God must teach.

So let us come down from the mountain above,
And share with them God's own true love.

Sand Castles

Children running along the beach, beside the ocean's shore,
Making castles out of sand, till the sun shines no more.
But the tide that rolls in at night will erase their art…
Which had been carefully put into place, made from their heart.
No matter how much work was done, through the course of that day,
The tide will always return, and remove their creation all away.

In life our dreams are like sand castles, that we build so high…
As we try to accomplish our goals, while reaching for the sky.
The changes in life that surprise us, always come around,
Breaking our world into pieces, causing it to fall down.

So we begin to lose touch with God, because of our fear,
And our trust in Him seems to fail, as we watch it disappear.
But we should let go of the temporary, and all life's tide has destroyed,
And focus on whatever is eternal, so God can restore our joy.

For even though we stand powerless, over whatever has to be,
We can be sure that God is in control, and His voice commands the sea.

The Hollow Heart

As this world changes from day to day, we encounter so much more,
   Material things are improved upon, even better than before.

Electronics, fashion wear, and even the cars we drive,
   No matter what we invent for ourselves, we are still dissatisfied.

For we want what others want, or we will simply die,
   But if we cannot have it all, we feel others have passed us by.

And if we get an expensive car, well to us, that's a big deal,
   But if our neighbor gets one better, how does that make us feel?

You see we are people of hollow hearts, who just cannot be pleased,
   And nothing in this earthly world can set our mind at ease.

So we must fill our hearts with God's Joy, Peace and Love,
   And seek first God's Kingdom and Heavenly things above.

Material things hold value, but they are disappearing fast,
   Only treasures of the heart from God, is what will truly last.

The Safest Place

Rumors of war are everywhere, with mass tragedy,
Fear of disease threatens many, with great catastrophe.
Death and terror surround us, as fear closes in.
Is there a safe place to go? Or is this the end?
Doom and gloom hang in the air, with every news cast,
Is there any help at all? For hope is fading fast.

There is one safe place that we can go, and it isn't far away,
Many will discover it, when they kneel and pray.
It isn't an old building, or a new one underground,
But it will provide shelter, once it has been found.
It always offers Peace and Amazing Grace,
Its security is sure, no matter what we face.

To find this place is simple, first one must believe,
For Jesus brings Salvation, to whoever will receive.
The safest place I'm referring to, is a hill called Calvary,
Where He died and shed His blood for you and me.
It offers us encouragement and restores our peace of mind,
Jesus is our Sanctuary, throughout the age of time.
So, let us trust in the Lord above, with our every prayer,
And let us pray others too, will find their refuge there.

To Encourage Others

Life bears down, with its cold iron hand,
It leaves us weak so we can barely stand.
Breaking us into pieces, with its stress and grief,
And we cry out, for some kind of relief.

We bury ourselves, in depression and sadness,
Till it gets the best of us and we go into madness.
Searching for something, we carry hope,
And we struggle, while trying to cope.

But if we could look beyond, the feeling of ourselves,
And take a look around us, we might see someone else.
Someone that if we meet, might exchange a smile,
And be our friend or can make us happy for a while.

Reaching out to someone in need, of our care,
Could perhaps make us feel useful, by just being there.
And if we show our best, even when we feel bad,
Sometimes gives us more, than what we already had.

For people watch people, in us they will find…
All that we choose to leave behind.
So, let them find some joy, which can be shared around,
And encourage someone else today, who might be feeling down.

To Suffer Rejection

You're sad, depressed and lonely, not wanting to go on,
Tears roll down your face, all your happiness is gone...

For no one seems to care for you, at least you feel this way,
No one cares to hear your plea, or what you have to say.

And so you continue to live your life, by only trying to cope,
But with all your shattered dreams, you cease to reach for hope.

Yet I know there is hope for you, so try to understand,
Although life has rejected you, someone is at hand.

That someone is Jesus, and He will accept you,
For when He lived upon the earth, He suffered rejection too!

He will accept you as you are, if on His name you call,
And He waits to give you, the Greatest Love of all.

Trapped Inside

Many years ago, it seems like yesterday,
You would cook me meals and care for me each day.

But now those days are gone, just a faded memory,
All is most forgotten, times that used to be.

Still, the greatest moment, I treasure most of all,
Is the time you taught me God's Word, when I was very small.

I still can hear you singing, the hymn "How Great Thou Art",
I miss your quiet prayers, that broke your gentle heart.

I bring up happy times, when I was just a kid,
I try hard to remind you of what your mind has hid.

But the more that I try, I see nothing left,
Of the "YOU", I once knew… now trapped inside yourself.

Sometimes I feel lost, disheartened and sad,
When I fail to recover, what we once had.

Your physical health, is as strong as it can be,
But your mind is gone, you no longer recognize me.

I feel at times I need you and don't know what to do,
I miss all the conversations; I use to have with you,

God's Love, His Word and promises are all you ever knew,
And now I too, must hold onto Him, as I muddle through.

I know His Love for me is constant and with me evermore,
Still, you are not here, at least not like before.

Yet, it is God that I cling to, through every trying hour,
Giving me the strength, for He is my Strong Tower.

Because with every visit, every smile, I still can see God's care,
And though you are trapped inside, He holds you safely there.

Troubled Thoughts

When misery loves company, it's easy for me to see,
All of my problems and focus is on me.

But gently I hear the Spirit, whisper to my heart,
Words of wisdom and love He has spoken from the start.

All sadness, disappointment or pain that I feel,
Is entrusted to God and His plan revealed.

Perhaps, not right away or anytime soon,
But one day at a time, my heart is attuned…

For the possibilities are so much more…
If I stop my complaining and whining galore.

My acts of kindness can give Glory to God,
By helping others out, as I travel a sod.

So go away troubled thoughts, I will not share,
Anymore of your time, that captures me there.

I have found a Love, that nothing can separate,
A life worth living, that God will consecrate.

I will give endless praise, unto my Lord,
And my heart will find its greatest reward.

Trust in God

To trust in God for our salvation, is that all we trust Him for?
Or does God expect us to trust Him, for a whole lot more.

How can we not trust God, for our daily little strife?
If we once trusted Him… to save our very life,

Is the time not quick enough, according to His Plan?
That makes us want to take matters, into our own hands.

Surely, the Lord who has saved our lowly Hell bound soul,
Can be trusted enough to give Him, complete control.

So many times we've failed Him, and showed no faith at all,
Because we didn't give to Him, our problems very small.

God doesn't weigh our strife, to see what's too heavy or light,
He just says cast all of our cares upon Him, and He will make things right.

When Bad Things Happen

When bad things happen, what do you do?
Are you fearful, angry or have attitude?

This life brings us change,
There are no guarantees,
For our health, jobs or families.

Trials are meant to grow us, bring us closer to God's design,
He is our Sanctifier as we are being refined.

When you feel frightened,
Does your fear increase?
Let God calm you for He is our Peace.

When you have no money,
And the bills are piling high,
Remember, the Lord is our Provider our needs He will supply.

If you've been trampled down,
Caught in a sinners lure,
Jesus is our Righteousness; He can make our lives pure.

If you have wandered away,
And can't find your way back home,
Jesus is the Shepherd who seeks you as you roam.

If you are sick,
Your body is tired and frail,
Pray to God our Healer that He will make you well.

If you find yourself abandoned,
You are now on your own,
Call unto the One who is God alone.

When bad things happen,
The future cannot foretell,
But God is always with us, our Immanuel.

So do not despair or give up hope,
Whatever circumstance should befall,
Just Praise Him, our Adonai, Jesus Lord of all.

When the Vows Have Been Broken

When the vows have been broken and the love is gone...
And the only music playing is a lonely night song...
Where do you go for comfort?

When the world you've lived in begins to change...
And your life is completely re-arranged...
Where is your stability?

Fear and sadness is the emotion you feel;
The pain you are going through is so unreal,
How do you find peace?

Rainbows of color for you have turned gray;
As it gets harder for you to face a new day,
Where is Your hope?

Bitterness is in your heart, tears in your eyes...
As you wonder what went wrong and you question... Why?
Who will help you out?

Jesus is the one who can...
He has restored the broken man.

His Love is dependable and won't disappoint you.
He can even give You back the joy you once knew.

But first you must be willing, to lay down at His feet,
Every trial and heartache that makes you reach defeat.

You must let go of all the sadness and depression in your soul,
And realize Jesus is the answer, by giving Him full control.

For He has the power to free this world from its sin,
And He will create in you the will to love again.

Why Do Bad Things Happen?

What words can someone say...
That will take the pain away?

What comfort can be shown...
That will erase the fears unknown?

For when bad things change our lives,
We all must question... Why?

And as circumstances rip into our soul...
Why can't we gain control?

Why do bad things happen? .... It's a question of the heart,
And there is easy answer, to keep us from falling apart.

But the suffering can be consoled, if in Christ we do believe,
And He will wipe away the tears, and our pain relieve...

For though we all must suffer, we suffer not alone,
And we will find the Hope in knowing, God is still on His Throne.

Windows of Light

A room full of darkness, I am hiding here,
Away from life's problems, thinking no one really cares.

The view is dismal and gray no hope can be seen,
A lonely, cold presence is felt, in everything.

Black curtains are hanging, as dark as can be,
No good thing is present no help do I see.

Shall I open a window, to receive a new view?
Perhaps, the air will be refreshing and the sky sea blue.

Birds may be singing a song for His Joy,
And I recall a time, when no one could destroy…

A day when my heart, was filled with Joy and Peace,
Yet today depression has me captive, with no hope of release.

But my prayers can uplift me with His Strength and His Power,
Regardless, of how I am feeling this hour.

The struggle within may be pulling me back,
But my God will help me in any attack.

So, I will open a window, a window of light,
And all darkness will be, chased into the night.

Words Cannot Express

Words cannot express,
The pain and unhappiness,
That you are feeling today.

For the loss of your loved one,
Has left you feeling numb,
And no one really knows what to say.

But in each miserable hour,
We can find Strength and Power,
Through Jesus Christ our King.

For He guides our destination,
He knows every frustration,
And He can soften our suffering.

I know the heartache that you feel,
Seems to you, to be unreal,
And you keep asking... Why?

But Christ is holding out His hand,
And He will surely help you stand,
If on His shoulder, you would like to cry.

And though it seems, you're on your own,
You do not have to be alone,
Jesus will help you through it all.

When others cannot help you out,
He will lift all of your doubts,
If on His name, you will only call.

Scripture References for Selected Poems
Chapter 6
THE TRUSTING TIME

The Trusting Time	Psalm 28:7
A Valentine of Praise	Matthew 5:4
As We Stand	Romans 5: 1-2
Fear and Fret Not	Psalm 34:4
God's Plan	Proverbs 16:2
God's Way	Isaiah 55: 8-9
I Cannot Feel	Matthew 11: 28-29
In the Clearing	Psalm 71:18
In the Suffering	Psalm 119:50
Just Remember	I Thessalonians 4: 13-18
Looking Beyond	2 Corinthians 4: 17-18
Panic Attack	Isaiah 26:3
Sand Castles	Psalm Chapter 46
The Hollow Heart	I Timothy 6: 6-12
To Encourage Others	I Thessalonians 5:14
To Suffer Rejection	Luke 6:22

If my people, who are called by my name, will humble themselves and pray and seek my face and turn from their wicked ways, then I will hear from heaven, and I will forgive their sin and will heal their land.

2 Chronicles 7:14

CHAPTER SEVEN

TAKE ANOTHER LOOK AMERICA

Take Another Look America

I'm proud to be an American, is what the people say,
But America is not the country, it used to be... today.
For we no longer have our freedom, and some may disagree,
But it seems America, is in captivity.

With violence like it is, among the harbor lights,
Gangs are running wild in the darkness of the night.
People are marching everywhere, to value once again.
What they think is right; to condone their own sin.

And drugs are flooding in so fast, without so much a plea,
Crime has reached the highest scale... is this our liberty?
Abortion is the answer, for running out of space,
Where nothing sacred such as life, has even left a trace.

There's unemployment everywhere, the rich and the poor,
Sex and child pornography is growing more and more.
How long will God Bless America, when we're the ones to blame,
To see how America has rebelled and cursed His Holy name.

I feel an empty feeling and almost a dreaded fear,
When I sing "God Bless America" I have to shed a tear.
Oh Lord! Have mercy on America, is what we all should cry,
Take another look Americans, or America will die.

America's Last Hope

What has happened to America, our land of the free?
For the one nation under God, is not what I see.
America is no longer the country it used to be before,
And most of its patriotism has been thrown out the door.
I wonder what went wrong, that could change our country so,
Could it be that America, just would not say NO.
For we didn't say no to the drugs, that were once not allowed,
And so they have taken over Americans, the strong and the proud.
Or maybe it's because we said no, to the value of human life,
When we made abortions legal, causing so much strife.
And let's not forget, that God created male and female,
And the sanctity of marriage, in His Holy detail.
The American dream is just that, a dream in reality,
With debts so high, that it must cut back social security.
And anyone trying to find, a job to make a wage,
Now, must seek the unemployment line at any given age.
Many businesses, are selling out their integrity,
American jobs are being outsourced, to foreign countries.
Our brave men and women have fought on foreign sand,
A war that has claimed many lives and seems to have no end.
Some leaders that we have put in charge, in our state capitol...
Show hidden agendas that may contribute to America's fall.
And the some of those sitting, in our congress chair,
Reveal public displays of a frivolous affair.
Many homes and offices have no boundaries,
From being posted on the internet, where everyone can see.
Technology soars, with knowledge that's all fluff,
In a failed economy, things are getting tough.
Perhaps we thought we were doing right, by pleasing everyone,
And so our moral standards have dropped, almost down to none.
So much has caused America to go bad,
But this one thing alone is what really makes me sad...
America has said no to God, in so many ways,
Like our public schools, where no one is allowed to pray.
By removing prayer, it has only sealed a child's doom.
Now they must deal with bombs and gunfire in the classroom,
I'm sure He is disappointed, as God watches from above,
God please bless America, oh this land I love!
As a nation we must return to Him, the One who loves us so,
And not make the mistake, Israel made many years ago.
Americans it's not too late, we still can change our ways,
If we as a nation will get down, on our knees and pray.
And ask God to lead our country, so that we will be able to cope,
God is the only One who can save us and He's America's last Hope.

Freedom for All

Yellow ribbons on display and patriotic tunes,
Everyone hoping the troops will be home soon.

Across the seas on the desert sands,
Fighting for freedom of our land.

Those who left their family and friends,
Are trying to ensure America a peaceful end.

Freedom for our country means some may not return,
So we suffer this loss as hearts will burn.

So it seems only right to remember at this time,
Another life laid down for the freedom of yours and mine.

For long ago, far beyond the seas,
Jesus was the first to die for you and me.

Taking our sins upon Him, He died on a cross,
So at this time let us count the cost...

Of all who have sacrificed themselves to make us free,
But the highest of all sacrifices was that at Calvary.

God's Country

God YOU are GOD and we are not,
Everything we have now, has cost us a lot.
For all the many blessings, we are thankful and unworthy,
With humbleness and reverence, You have shown us great mercy.

It seems this country has forgotten who You are,
It saddens me to know we are so far.
It's ironic to me, that we celebrate each year,
When the shackles are visible and captivity is clear.

For if this country were truly free,
It's not by our own humanity,
We spend our money like there is more,
And our debts are higher than ever before.

America has deteriorated, into a foul decay,
No one understands brotherhood, in the right way.
Morals are declining, for our future generations,
Schools are being searched, in dire situations.

Many documentaries and studies search out Your existence,
But Your Truth rarely surfaces, without their resistance.
All the beauty You've created, has been stolen as man's own,
While scientists have tried making many different clones.

What a mess we have made, of this country and your world,
We are all accountable, for the innocence of each boy and girl.
But Praise God, there is still hope for us, if we will only pray,
And with broken hearts, fall on our knees today.

Then You will hear our prayers and Salvation you will send,
Only then, will America be "God's Country" again.

The Empty Playground

One night I dreamt, I was in Heaven, walking on the streets of gold,
Reuniting with those, who had gone on before, the young and the old.

Then Jesus took my hand, and softly said to me,
"Welcome to My Kingdom, there is so much to see".
He showed me the gates of pearl, and I heard the angel's choir,
Giving Praise to the One, that they most desired.

I saw the Tree of Life, and the Crystal Sea,
Nothing was as I had imagined, or expected it would be.
As I continued to take my tour, looking all around,
I began to hear laughter, from a children's playground.

Yet this playground was empty, no child could be seen,
And this appeared to be, a very strange thing...

So I asked God about it, and it brought a tear to His eye,
"This is the only unhappy part of Heaven", He said with a sigh.
"For this place was meant for every child, to play in one day,
But so many never got the chance, because man had his way".

"Little baby boys and girls would have been blessed by me,
But they were given a death sentence, where no one heard their plea".
"I had such plans for them, so My Message they might hear,
But man thought he knew best, and so he chose to interfere".

"Man felt he could do without, the children's laughter and joy,
And so decided to take the lives, of many girls and boys".
"And since man didn't need or want, these little ones around,
Their souls will remain with Me, here in this empty playground".

Suddenly, I awakened from this dream, with sweat upon my face,
And I started to realize the shame and disgrace...
So, we need to value the rights of those, inside the womb and out!
Abortion in this world, was what my dream was about,

For if we don't save the unborn child, that we choose to kill,
It could one day make this dream come true and the empty playground real.

The Folded Flag

You wore your uniform with Honor, your medals with dignity,
You fought for America's freedom, you protected her Liberty.

You sent many letters back home to us,
While encouraging your brothers in war,

You carried out every command you were given,
As you gave back to others, even more.

I don't have any answers now, while we are standing here,
Staring at this folded flag, through heavy eyes of tears.

But I know that God watched over you, and He heard every prayer,
Even though the gunfire and bombs, created a smoke filled air…

Perhaps, it happened in an instant, with little pain at all,
Or maybe you struggled for a while, as past memories you did recall.

But in that stolen moment… where life flashed before your eyes,
I know you felt God's Hand, reach down from the skies.

You had all the courage of a soldier, your bible at your chest,
And with Jesus as your Savior, you died in peaceful rest.

So, now may we gain Wisdom, from God above on High,
To grant us all His Mercy, as so many have had to die.

Oh let us always remember these, with their stories as we brag,
In loving memory as we treasure…

Our Freedom's Folded Flag.

True American Way

You served in the military for our country,
Your destination was Iraq,
As you fought the gunfire and bombings,
You questioned if you would come back...

Many days and nights you missed home,
And all the people you loved most,
Yet, it wasn't enough of a priority,
For you to ever leave your post...

As you fought for our country,
You felt there was more to do,
So, you reached out to the Iraqi people,
While encouraging, your unit too...

After all that time of waiting,
Within that nowhere land,
You were consistent, faithful and strong,
With each strategic plan...

The enemy had to be stopped,
And this war could not end,
Until everyone had a place to live,
Where Freedom was their friend...

We prayed for you each night and day,
For God to once again,
Bring you safely home,
To your family and friends...

So, we wanted you to know,
In this very special way,
We thank you for protecting us
In a True American Way.

What Will It Take

Was it not enough to suffer the loss?
Our Savior bled upon the cross.
Was it not enough to forgive our sin?
When our Lord was despised and beaten by men.
Was it not enough for us to forgive?
Wrongs done to us as we daily live.

Yes, it was enough and we should know...
Hate, anger and grudges that grow...
Are displeasing to God and defy His Name!
Can we really say we are not ashamed?

The ones who ignored His Plea,
He died to set THEM free.
Are we so blind that we can't see?
That we are all guilty!
And now the devil dances here,
Upon our silent stubborn fears...
While our Jesus sheds a tear,
Waiting patiently near...

What will be the cost this hour?
What will take away this selfish power?
Will it be distance as time slips away?
Will it be isolation or another bad day?
What will it take? Oh I pray not the call,
Of disaster, crisis or death to break down these walls...
For life is too short to leave it undone,
With hearts divided between loved ones.

We say another day, another time or maybe tomorrow,
Yet have we not seen this year... the unexpected sorrow?
Make it right today for our lives on earth are like grass...
One day we are here but it will not last.

Jesus spoke of forgiveness in the Bible so True,
He said "If you do not forgive them, I cannot forgive you."
"If you have fought with another, go and make it right,
And do not allow your anger to keep through the night".

So what will it take to obey God's Words...?
By being a doer of what we have heard.
Harsh words, hurt feelings, they do matter, I am sure...
But Forgiveness, Mercy and Love are the Cure.

Scripture References for Selected Poems
Chapter 7
TAKE ANOTHER LOOK AMERICA

Take Another Look America	2 Chronicles 7:14
America's Last Hope	Psalm 33: 10-15
The Folded Flag	Psalm Chapter 23
Freedom for All	2 Corinthians 3:17
God's Country	Proverbs 29:2
The Empty Playground	Psalm 139: 13-16
True American Way	Psalm 20: 1-7
What Will It Take	Colossians 3:13

Take Another Look America

The unfolding of your words gives light;

it gives understanding to the simple.

Psalm 119:130

CHAPTER EIGHT

MORE THAN STORIES

More than Stories

These stories that I tell, that have a simple rhyme,
Are more than just fables of some created time.

They resonate a Truth so pure, that teach a Love so True,
Yes, these are more than stories, that I write for me and you.

Stories of God's Love and guidance at its best,
To help us all live our lives and pass the daily tests.

Stories that will challenge us and provide a fresh start,
For the Truth from God's Word, which can change any heart.

Jesus too, used stories in the parables He'd share,
All with the message, to show others God's Care.

It is my prayer that you will see Jesus in each one,
And feel His Love for you, before the day is done.

Final Touches

A small stone lying in the ground all dusty and old,
Hardly one would recognize this small piece was gold.

For it had been wasting away under God's green earth,
Until a miner took it home, he thought it was of worth.

The miner felt that this would be a way to make his trade,
But before it would sell, a price had to be paid.

So, he threw it in the fire, life's greatest test,
Always knowing in the end, he would have the best.

He later retrieved it from the heat and the burning coal,
To find a beauty so enlightening, that all would behold.

So many times as Christians, we often bear the pain,
Of being thrown into the fire, by the world's domain.

God found us wasting away, just as the stone,
So He rescued us, to keep us for His own.

But before He could save us, a price had to be paid,
That's when God sent His Son, so a way for us was made.

Sometimes God will test us, according to His Will,
He Tests every part of us, to see if our faith is real.

He wants to be our Anchor, through the tough times that we face,
Teaching us to rest in His Strength, His Love and His Grace.

He wants us to always trust in Him, as we walk through life's fire,
So He can safely lift us out, onto mountains that are higher.

Then someday after these trials are over, His face we shall surely see,
And the final touches of our lives will be revealed, as God's complete Creativity.

Genuine Love

Several years ago, while panning for gold,
Another discovery was found, we are told...
Something so similar, to gold was seen,
Yet, it wasn't the exact same thing.

It shined like gold, and glittered around,
It too had been lying, beneath the ground.
It was just an imitation, worthless even though,
Many people were fooled, by its radiant glow...

There are many times as Christians, we often display,
The same kind of beauty, that has an array,
When we offer our help, and pretend that we care,
But the motive of love, is really not there.

And just like the gold, others are fooled by our charm...
When we put on a show, that sometimes causes harm.
Even though we act humble, and try to be kind,
This is not what others, are looking to find.

People are searching, for a Genuine Love,
Like that of Jesus, who came from above.
A Love that is true, and full of hope, that is real,
Because we are a mirror, of what our heart feels.

And if we are authentic, by what we say and do,
Then people will know, the real me and you.
For as Christians in this world, we have been set apart,
So that others may see Jesus, inside of our heart.

Hog Heaven

Many years ago, there once was a young man,
That went his own way, away from his home land.
So he gathered all that belonged to him, and left happily,
To discover and experience, all he could see.

At first it was great, as he started on his way,
He was in "Hog Heaven", and he wanted to stay.
At first he dined with the best, and didn't have a doubt,
But soon a famine came to the land, and his money ran out.

He found himself alone, trying to survive,
And so he worked out in the field, just to stay alive.
His duties were to feed the swine, and the same food he ate,
Many regrets did he have, but now it was too late.

But, suddenly he remembered, all he had left behind,
So he went back home, in hopes that he would find…
His father's forgiveness and love's open door,
Because he didn't want to live, in "Hog Heaven" anymore.

Perhaps like the prodigal, you have also found,
That certain "Hog Heaven", that seems to be around.
It fools us into thinking, that we can have it all,
But it only lures us into, a much greater fall.

For when we stray away from God, to try the world's domain,
We are only asking for, more unnecessary pain.
And when we leave for something more, we only find less,
Because we do not realize, with God we have the best.

So, if you are in "Hog Heaven", and don't know what to do…
Just arise, and go back home, for your Father waits for you.

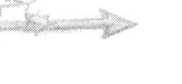

In God's Hand

A mother sparrow left her nest, hoping she would find,
Some food to feed her baby birds that she'd left behind.
But later when she returned, with her motherly care,
She found her little baby birds, were no longer there.

In fear she flew from tree to tree, in search for her young,
But they were nowhere to be found, and the day was done.
All through the night the mother sparrow, waited in concern,
Hoping that her baby birds would have a safe return.

Then suddenly, she heard a chirp, so she flew down to see,
And there were her baby birds, as safe as could be.
So amazed she began to realize, that they had not been alone,
For she had found, that God knew best, and He took care of His own.

So many times like the mother sparrow, we are torn apart,
When we worry about the ones, who are precious to our heart.
Circumstances that we can't handle tear at our fragile soul,
And we cease to believe, that God is still in control.

So in despair we search to find, the answers out our self,
But by doing this we only set, God upon the shelf.
For He is there to help us out, in our needed hour,
And when we put our faith in Him, we find His Strength and Power.

So we must always trust in Him, and then we will understand,
That God watches over the ones we love, as He holds them in His hand.

Out of the Nest

As a mother eagle taught her young to fly,
She sailed through the air and soared through the sky.
She hoped to encourage them, by her display,
So they would want to try it, on their own someday.

But as the young eaglets, watched her take flight,
They became restless and full of great fright.
For they were as content, as they felt they should be,
And they didn't want to give up, their security.

At once the mother eagle, started to destroy,
All that they had, in their nest of joy.
And they were all made, to quickly jump out,
So they could experience, what life was about.

As Christians God wants to teach us His best,
But we must be willing, to leave our nest.
And since God expects from us, so much more,
We must first learn how to fly, in order that we may soar.

But if we become comfortable, and we limit ourselves,
Then we are setting God's teachings, upon a shelf.
And so He is forced, to destroy the nests of our life,
Which can throw us out, in great heartache and strife.

We should never be willing, to settle down…
When we have the ability to reach, higher planes of ground.
And if there ever comes a time, when we should start to fall,
Know that God's Wings of Grace will carry us all.

To all those who are afraid, let your heart sing,
For God is our Strength and wind beneath our wings.

Removing the Masks

An invitation was sent out, one day to everyone,
To join in a celebration, of masquerading fun.
And so when the guests arrived, wearing costumes of their best,
No one could tell who they really were, or even tried to guess.
Later that night, they had to remove, their masks as a rule,
And to their surprise and disbelief, they all had been fooled.

Sometimes it can be so much fun, to put on a different face,
But in our relationships of everyday, this should not be the case.
For when we pretend to be something we're not, then we are not being fair,
And other people are being deceived, by something that is not there.
But God expects us to reflect who we are, from the inside and out,
For when we are honest with those we know, it won't leave room for doubt.

You see, when we display God's perfect Love, then Joy it will bring,
So let us remove any masks we wear, so others can see the real thing.

The Lighthouse

There is an old house, by the seaside,
That stands so tall, against the tide,
It shows a light, so it may be,
Guidance to the ones at sea.

It never fails to show its light,
To ships that pass by, through the night.
It saved one ship, and many more,
This old house, by the shore.

Well, this brings my story to an end,
But please consider this my friend...
Each one of us are ships at sail,
That need be guided away from hell.

The world is like the tempest sea,
That makes it hard for you and me.
But wait this isn't the end of the line,
We also have a Light which shines.

Jesus is our Light, call on Him and be saved,
Those of you, who are tossed by the waves,
For if He sees, your ship by night,
He will surely, show you the Light.

The Sparrow

God made a sparrow and gave it life,
And tried to keep it from much strife.
He stretched forth His hands to guide its wings,
But the sparrow wanted other things.

And when the sparrow was strong enough to fly,
It wasn't grateful and said goodbye.
So it soon chose its own way to soar,
And thought it was happy like never before.

But one day as it was flying around,
A skillful shooter shot it down.
It cried and wailed and felt it was nothing,
But God gave it strength so it could be something.

And the sparrow asked God, "Why did this happen to me?"
And God said that it was plain to see…
'You left me for all the rest,
When here with me, you had the best.
You took your wings so high above,
That you forgot your first love'.

So many times this story is true,
With life that deals with me and you.
We often fail, like the sparrow each day,
When we want to go, each our own way.
And even though we fail and wander in sin,
He picks us up for He is our friend.

But we should stay close by His side,
And let Him be our only guide.

The Traveler and the Follower

One day a man started out, walking down a road so long,
On his back was a heavy load, but he left singing a song.
As he journeyed down the path, his footsteps became weak,
He began to run out of breath, and could hardly speak.

But despite the trouble; he still trudged on his way,
With full confidence, he would make it one day.
When finally he became so weary, that he had to stop,
So he sat down on the ground, and his face began to drop.

So disgusted with himself, he gave up and cried,
But suddenly someone, was standing by his side...
"I've been following you for hours", said another voice,
"I wanted to help you with your load sooner, but I had no choice.
I had to wait until you rested, on this rugged route,
And now that I've caught up with you, I can finally help you out".

Many times as people, we find in our life,
We bear a load of struggles, and carry a load of strife.
Yet God wants to help us, but we first must understand,
That we have to give up our load, in order to see God's Hand.

For He's waiting there to help us out, in our time of need,
But we are so self-confident, He cannot intercede.
We think we can make it on our own strength, but we often fall,
Because we are so far away, we cannot hear His call.

Therefore, it's in our own failure, that we can finally see,
God's Hand stretched out reaching for us, in answer to our plea.
So, it's in the story of the traveler, that we come to find,
That the One who wants to help us, has been left behind.

Scripture References for Selected Poems
Chapter 8
MORE THAN STORIES

More Than Stories	Psalm 119:30
Genuine Love	I John 4: 7-10
Hog Heaven	Luke 15: 11-24
In God's Hand	Psalm 46:1
Out of the Nest	Isaiah 40: 28-31
The Lighthouse	John 8:12
The Sparrow	Matthew 10: 29-31
The Traveler and the Follower	Matthew 11: 28-30

But encourage one another daily, as long as it is called "Today," so that none of you may be hardened by sin's deceitfulness.

Hebrews 3:13

CHAPTER NINE

SIMPLE POEMS

Simple Poems

Sometimes, we need the simple poems with their silly little rhymes,
That bring a smile to our face amidst the heavy times.

Birthday wishes, or an occasion to share,
Send a few words of encouragement to let others know we care.

Or maybe a get well prayer to someone who is ill,
Whatever the reason or the time a poem can fit the bill.

So, I hope these poems I have written will help you not forget,
Others are waiting to be caught in our fisher's net.

Some are lost and some are found but at the end of the day,
We can show them the Love of God in the smallest way.

A Friend Like You

A friend like you, is very few, and very far between,
As through your care for people, God's Love is always seen.

For all the encouragement, you've given me, has made a true display,
Of a kind, generosity, that directs others to His Way.

And since your life has made a special mark, upon the life I live,
I now would like to extend, the same consideration that you give.

By letting you know how I feel, with all I say and do,
As I give God my thankfulness, for sending a friend like you.

Every Remembrance of You (A Poem of Friendship)

Many days in my life have been brightened, others not so bright,
Many nights I fought the darkness, while searching for the light.
Situations would often take me, for a very costly ride,
Sometimes they left my disheartened soul so un-satisfied.

So seeing me in despair, the Lord looked upon me one day,
And arranged a special blessing, by sending you my way,
Sharing God's Love with you, and giving Him sweet praise,
Has given me meaning in the solitary days.

For two are better than one, as someone has said before,
And two Christians serving God, account for so much more.
God allowed the opportunity, for us to become friends,
And the Christian bond that we have, will never have to end.

For it is a spiritual bond between us, and though we must part,
God has given us His Son, and He connects our hearts.
And we can be reassured in times, when we do not understand,
That God is faithful and He holds the situation in His hand.

So as I say goodbye, let me also say this too,
May my thanks be unto God, for every remembrance of you.

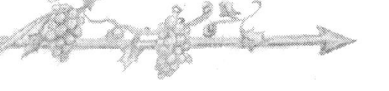

For the Graduate

You've grown to be a fine young person for everyone to see,
Eager for the future and what is meant to be.

So, since you are graduating I'll pray for you today,
And I'll offer you some advice that I've learned along the way.

Always be kind to others when they are not kind to you,
For someday, they might need your help on knowing what to do.

Be dedicated to your career and loyal to your friends,
It's in the challenging moments that you'll find real life begins.

Remember your teachers and others, who have brought you to this place,
Always extend your heart and hand, with God's Loving Grace.

Don't forget the early days of your childhood years,
Be courageous and confident; do not hide behind your fears.

Relax and don't stress out but have some fun too!
And should you ever need some help, God will see you through.

Ma

I never knew her very well,
But others did, who always tell,
Of Ma's loving, tender ways,
Of whom she was in older days.

Stories that would make you cry,
Or make you shout aloud,
Times that will never die,
And would certainly make you proud.

Stories that were told to me,
Memories so clear,
In ways I can imagine,
As if Ma was right here.

One thing that was impressed upon me,
That I most adored,
Was the way she loved her family,
And how she loved the Lord.

For when troubles crept upon her,
And sorrows often came,
She would fall on her knees and pray,
Asking everything in His Name.

Her faith was very strong,
Those of very few,
And In the raising of her children,
She depended on God to see her through.

She would kneel by their bed,
To pray by their side,
Then she would listen to their prayers,
And I'm sure she often cried.

As her children tell these stories from their heart,
I know this Love comes from God and it will never part.
So now, I thank God for her upon my bended knee,
For the same Love she taught her children,
Was also taught to me.

New Year's Resolution

Let's make a resolution that will help us to be,
Kinder to others and the people we see,
Always remember that God created this earth,
It is for us to enjoy and value its worth.

Take time to admire the beautiful flowers,
For in them you will see time's stolen hours,
Of the beauty and splendor this world holds,
As we live each moment and the years unfold.

We live each moment to its fullest part,
So, let us continue to keep God in our heart.
May we draw closer to Him, each and every day,
As God's Blessings enrich our life, with all that comes our way.

Pa

We will not say goodbye,
Despite the tears we cry,
To the man that we loved so.

Perhaps one day… you saw,
Our dear departed Pa,
Walking down the street, when he felt low.

Walking was a way,
He would start a brand new day,
To sort through the plans of his life.

Though times weren't always good,
He did the best he could,
For those he loved and especially his wife.

Now Pa was one, who talked,
About his daily walks,
To his grand-children and those he knew.

He would often say,
When you walk alone someday,
You've got to know what to do.

So, if Pa were here today,
I know just what he'd say,
"I am not in pain anymore".

"Someday I'll see you all,
For those who have heard God's call,
As we walk together down Heaven's Shore."

Teach Me

Teach me Lord to be watchful and to see other's needs,
Teach me to be careful, in what life I may lead.

Teach me to be honest and do Your good will,
Teach me to be caring, for those who are ill.

Teach me to be compassionate, on those who need prayer,
Teach me to extend the love that encourages me to share.

Teach me to love even those who hate me,
Teach me to understand what has to be.

Teach me to be thankful in all that I do,
But most of all Lord... Teach me to remember, My Teacher was You.

Thank You

Someone to depend on... is what we all need,
And make time for us... with a kind word or deed.

You are that someone... who came through for me,
By displaying your heart... of what all people should be.

So I just thought I would write this... to express my gratitude,
And please let me know... if I can ever help you.

The Lives We Touch Are Many

As the stars number the sky… and twinkle with God's Light,
May He bless us richly… with His Presence of Delight,
As we take the time to see… what beauty this world holds,
May He grant us wisdom… with each moment that unfolds.

May we live each moment… to its fullest part,
Giving, sharing and showing… God's Love from our hearts.
The lives we touch are many… though we may not understand,
The impact we can have… with our Father's Hand…

As blessings enrich our life… with all that comes our way,
Let us be a blessing to others, each and every day.

The Silver Years

Though your eyes are dimmed and your hearing is very low,
The words you say are mixed and your steps are kind of slow.

The wisdom and the wonder can still be seen in you,
As you tell the many stories like you often do.

Stories of your childhood days still fresh in your mind,
Memories of such value are hard to leave behind.

And though you may not recollect just who, when or where,
Others who know you remember the stories that they share.

So, may God watch over you and bless you every day,
For all the pleasure you have brought in every kind of way.

Scripture References for Selected Poems
Chapter 9
SIMPLE POEMS

Simple Poems	Hebrews 3:13
Every Remembrance of You	Philippians 1:3
For the Graduate	Proverbs 16:9
Ma	Hebrews 12:1
Teach Me	Psalm 25: 4-5

People were bringing little children to Jesus for him to place his hands on them, but the disciples rebuked them. When Jesus saw this, he was indignant. He said to them, "Let the little children come to me, and do not hinder them, for the kingdom of God belongs to such as these. Truly I tell you, anyone who will not receive the kingdom of God like a little child will never enter it." And he took the children in his arms, placed his hands on them and blessed them.

Mark 10: 13-16

CHAPTER TEN

JUST A KID

Just a Kid

You may think I'm just a kid but you cannot see,
That deep inside my heart something has happened to me.

For Jesus is now my Savior and watches me with care,
He is here with me, hearing my prayers.

So, please don't call me just a kid, because one day I'll be…
Living with the King for I am royalty.

A Child's Smile

Dear Lord, we see so much of you,
Within children and all that they do.

Their smile reaches our hearts with love,
It touches us, from Heaven above.

When we hear their laughter as quietly they play,
It reminds us of the joy, that fills our houses each day.

Even in the moments, when times are very hard,
We know everything is okay, with You standing guard.

It sometimes gets rough, but they seem to muddle through,
Always to see each blessing, comes straight from you.

And nothing is as beautiful, as the sound in the night,
Than their soft little prayers, near a tiny night-light.

So thank-you for their tender lives, displayed for all to see,
All they were, all they are and all they hope to be.

A Tiny Little Light

A tiny little light,
Can brighten a night,
As it scatters the darkness away...

But a Heavenly Glow,
Will let someone know,
That Jesus is the Way!

Afraid of the Dark

I use to be afraid of what I could not see,
That might be living in the dark, always watching me.

So, I would fall asleep, leaving on the light,
To keep away the bad things, that bothered me at night.

Until one day my mom told me, that Jesus too was there,
Watching over me, with all His Love and Care.

So now when I'm afraid, I get on my knees and pray,
And all the things that scare me, quickly go away.

Daniel

Daniel was a man, who would always pray,
Unto his God, three times a day.

But the king was fooled, into writing a decree,
That couldn't be changed, so you see…

Some evil men, set up a plot,
And trapped Daniel, so that he would be caught…

Praying to His God quietly in his room…
And it seemed Daniel would be doomed.

Those evil men, were not Daniel's friends…
So Daniel was thrown, into the lion's den.

But even then, he prayed while there…
And God did answer, Daniel's prayer.

God closed the lion's mouth and Daniel was saved,
And the next day the King went, to see if he was okay.

Daniel told the king, what God had done,
Then the king proclaimed GOD, as the only One.

Next the king said, to find those evil men,
And this time they were thrown, into the lion's den.

And so the lions, did fiercely attack,
And they had a very, tasty snack.

David and Goliath

When David was a boy, he was small like me,
But he killed a giant, for everyone to see,
The giant's name was Goliath and he was a Philistine,
Who hated God and His People; He was very mean.

David heard Goliath making fun, of God's name,
And so he took his sling shot and swung it with great aim.
The stone hit Goliath and so he fell down,
And everyone was watching, while standing all around.

Then David went over and cut off Goliath's head,
And everyone was happy because Goliath was now dead.

God's Greenhouse

There once was a little flower, that in a garden grew,
Underneath the sunshine, and the sky so blue.
People passing by, had to stop and stare,
At its color bright and its beauty fair.

The little flower was happy, and content as could be,
And every day it stood so tall, for everyone to see.
But one night a winters storm, brought heavy rain and snow,
And the howling wind beat and blew, against the flower so.
But suddenly it was rescued, from the raging storm,
And placed in a greenhouse, where it could be kept warm.

As Christians we can relate, to this story told,
When we are kept safe and warm, against the bitter cold.
For the world often beats us down, with its cruel demands,
But then our Father picks us up, with His gentle loving hands.
He protects us in His care, so we can rise above,
Giving Him Glory, as we grow, in God's greenhouse of Love.

Heaven

Heaven is so far away,
But I am going there someday...

To live with Jesus, my best friend,
A place where time where will never end...

You can also come along,
And we will sing a happy song.

JESUS

He was born a child of innocence,
He preached in a temple so good.

He died on a cross filled with violence,
He shed His most precious blood.

He's giving us a chance to live, with Him for eternity,
For the only reason He died, was for you and me.

His tender hands they lead me, His voice I've heard Him call...
Take up thy cross and follow me, for I have paid it all.

Little Butterflies

Little butterflies and birds in the air,
Fly so very high, without a tiny care...

Of falling from the sky or any little thing,
God takes care of them and guides their little wings...

And as they fly all around, for everyone to see,
I know God is watching and taking care of me.

Lullaby Prayer

Dear Lord, guard this little one as he sleeps tonight,
May he feel Your presence and know everything is alright.

If he awakens, in the middle of the dawn,
Hush his crying, with a Heavenly song.

If he fears the darkness and doesn't understand,
Quiet him with peace, with a touch of Your hand.

Watch over this child, in every kind of way,
All he may do, all he will say,

As we give You praise, for all that You do,
Praying this child, will one day know You too.

Lunch Break

The bible tells a story, that happened long ago,
As Jesus taught the people and the crowd began to grow.
The crowd was hungry but no one, had brought anything to eat,
Soon everyone was restless, as they gathered by the sea.

So Jesus showed compassion and He asked his disciples this...
"What can we feed these people?" But this was just a test...
Jesus already knew the answer, of what He was going to do,
So he sat everyone down, among the multitude.

Then Andrew, Peter's brother, found a small little lad,
But five loaves and two fishes, were all that he had.
Andrew told Jesus, "This isn't much?"
But Jesus took and blessed the little boy's lunch.

Then after the people were full, with very happy tummies,
Twelve baskets were gathered, with leftover yummies.
And now no one was hungry, because of Heaven's sake,
From Jesus' feeding miracle and a special lunch break.

Momma Tells Me

Momma tells me about Jesus, every night and day,
And He watches over me, in every kind of way.

She says if I have a problem, I should talk to Him in prayer,
And He can hear me praying, since He is everywhere.

So I'm very happy and in my heart there's joy,
Because Momma tells me Jesus, loves every girl and boy.

Piggy Bank

My piggy bank is full, it sits on my shelf,
All the coins inside I saved by myself.

I've been saving all my nickels, pennies and dimes,
For something really special and now is the time.

I'm not going to spend this money in the mall,
Or spend it on a fancy toy or pretty baby doll.

This money won't be spent on a toy that can fly,
Or a cool shiny bike, that I can go ride.

I won't be using it, to buy something sweet,
My money isn't for, anything to eat.

My money has a purpose, that isn't for a store,
It helps little kids like me, learn about Jesus more.

And someday when I see Jesus, I'll also hope to see,
All of them in Heaven, together there with me.

The Devil

An angel was kicked out of heaven one day,
I know this may sound odd...

And the reason it happened, was because,
He thought he was better than God...

He was the most beautiful angel,
Of all the angels you could know...

Lucifer was his name,
And he tried to run the show...

He had so much pride in his heart,
God said he had to dwell...

In the depths below earth,
A place called Hell.

So the moral of this story,
That really ought to be said...

Pride comes from the Devil,
So don't get a big head.

The Lamb and the Wolf

One day a little lamb, was walking in the field,
Along with other sheep, on a clover hill.
But on the other side, of the hill so green,
Lived a hungry wolf, which was very mean.

This wolf stared at the lamb, all through the day,
As he tried to think up, a very clever way...
To get across on the other side, to eat the little lamb,
And so he thought up the smartest way, to pull off his scam.

"I'll dress up like the sheep", the mean ole wolf replied,
"And the real sheep won't know, it's truly me inside."
Then the wolf crossed over the hill, so very smooth and sly,
And the other sheep didn't recognize, a wolf had passed them by.

He went over to the little lamb, and said "How are you?
I would like to be your friend, will you be mine, too?"
'Why sure', the little lamb said, 'Let us have some fun',
But the little lamb didn't realize, what the wolf had done.

"Let us go over there" the wolf said, "And get out of this heat",
For the wolf was hungry and the lamb he wanted to eat.
And when the wolf had took off, the clever sheep disguise,
The little lamb was fearful, for he had been surprised.

So the little lamb had been fooled, by what had not been real,
And the wolf did eat the little lamb, for his only meal.
You see this may be just a story, but we can often see,
A little of the wolf and lamb, within you and me.

People that we care about, sometimes use our kindly heart,
To only get to the other side, so that they can tear us apart.
So we must watch for the wolves... dressed like sheep, and always be aware,
Of all the things that are not of God... that will bring us great despair.

Telling the Truth

By telling lies it makes it hard to know…
When what is being said, is really so?

When people are not truthful, it makes it hard you see,
To ever really know if what is – is to be.

We should always be honest every single day,
So others will be able, to believe the words we say.

Scripture References for Selected Poems
Chapter 10
Just A Kid

Just a Kid	Mark 10: 13-16
A Tiny Little Light	Matthew 5: 14-16
Afraid of the Dark	Psalm 139:12
Daniel	Daniel Chapter 6
David and Goliath	I Samuel Chapter 17
Jesus	Matthew 1:21
Lunch Break	John 6: 1-14
Momma Tells Me	Deuteronomy 6: 5-7
Piggy Bank	Matthew 6: 19-21
The Devil	Isaiah 14: 12-15
The Lamb and the Wolf	Matthew 7:15
Telling the Truth	Proverbs 12:19

And there were in the same country shepherds abiding in the field, keeping watch over their flock by night. And, lo, the angel of the Lord came upon them, and the glory of the Lord shone round about them: and they were sore afraid. And the angel said unto them, Fear not: for, behold, I bring you good tidings of great joy, which shall be to all people. For unto you is born this day in the city of David a Saviour, which is Christ the Lord. And this shall be a sign unto you; Ye shall find the babe wrapped in swaddling clothes, lying in a manger. And suddenly there was with the angel a multitude of the heavenly host praising God, and saying, Glory to God in the highest, and on earth peace, good will toward men.

Luke 2:8-14 (KJV)

CHAPTER ELEVEN

THE GIFT OF CHRISTMAS

The Gift of Christmas

Christmas is not just singing carols of joy,
Or buying a child a brand new toy.
Though it can be seen in many ways,
There is so much more to this Holiday.

Christmas is not the presents we buy,
It's not the snow that falls from the sky,
It's not found in Santa or his jolly elves…
It's not at the North Pole or on the store shelves.

It's the Love that comes from God's own heart,
To us the greatest treasure He did impart.
Christmas the gift, God's own son,
Is Jesus… the Messiah and Holy One.

So trim your trees and deck the halls,
But just remember one and all.
Christmas is Jesus, God's Truth rings clear,
Let us spread the message to those far and near.

For joy, peace and love is what we all can share,
Through heartfelt compassion as we show others we care.
Then it will reach every man, woman, boy and girl,
And Peace and Goodwill shall cover this world.

A Christmas Encouragement

Candy canes are sweet, striped with red and white,
Pine cones fill our homes with a fragrance of delight.
Jingle bells ring out announcing Christmas cheer...
Reminding us all of this special time of year.

And so I want to wish you a happy holiday,
To encourage your heart in a very special way.
Not just with gifts or ornaments to decorate your tree...
But by sharing with you what Christmas means to me.

CHRISTMAS is JESUS ... when God became man.
Here on earth, He gave His Life so all would understand,
It's a relationship with God that only He can create.
JESUS is the One who offers Love, Joy and Hope...
He is only a prayer away from a world that cannot cope.

He offers us redemption to free us from our sin,
A True Reflection of Christmas and Peace, Goodwill to men.
So it is my prayer for you... and I hope that you will see,
CHRISTMAS is a SAVIOR ... sent for you and me.

Christmas in the Real World

Tis the Season for great joy, tis a time of peace,
Yet today the anger lies, within the hidden streets.
Christmas pines standing tall decorated in red and gold,
Do not seem as beautiful, to the homeless in the cold.

Children singing Christmas carols, through their neighborhoods,
Is simply not advised, for the sake of their own good.
People shuffling everywhere, going mall to mall,
Must secure their articles or thieves will take it all.

Tis the Season to be jolly, to everyone we know,
Except for those who hold a grudge, be he friend or foe.
Some charities who offer help, with their Christmas cheer,
Is just to families they have selected, only once a year.

To the depressed, suicide seems the only way,
So, what does CHRISTMAS really mean... for anyone today?

After all these many years, since our Lords birth,
Not a lot has really changed, on this sinful earth.
For even on that HOLY night, despair was all around,
As Joseph and expectant Mary, moved back to their home town.

They arrived from their journey, exhausted, tired and worn,
And there amongst all the confusion, baby Jesus was born.
Many try to glamorize, the whole manger scene,
But these were terrible circumstances, for a Holy King.

But the fact that Jesus came, to this world of loss,
And later suffered at the hands of men, upon a cruel cross,
Proves the very LOVE of God, in which we celebrate,
Not just a time of Christmas, but for a SAVIOR whose HEART is great!

The Perfect Gift

What good is a Christmas without Jesus, as the center of our Joy?
What is the use of giving material things, that will one day be destroyed?

What precious gift can we give, that will last throughout the years?
A prayer of Hope, a word of Love and wipe away some tears.

Do a kind deed, be a friend in need and encourage someone this day,
Tell of the Savior who loves them... For He is the Truth, the Life and the Way!

A Gift like this cannot be bought or could ever become lost,
No, for it is found, given and enjoyed, within the Glory of the Cross!

Spreading Tidings

Mistletoe in the hall,
Giving gifts to One and all,

Sharing love with those on earth,
While celebrating our Lord's birth...

So often as this time draws near,
We always spread the yuletide cheer...

But when the Holiday, has passed us by,
Our Christmas spirit seems to die.

But if we keep this joy in our hearts,
Then Christmas will not depart,

For Christmas begins with me and you,
Let's make it last the whole year through.

The True Meaning of Christmas

Long before the halls were decked or any carols sung...
Way before the tree was trimmed or any stockings hung,
God had a plan...

Love would be the answer. Peace would come to earth...
A joyful celebration! Announcing Jesus birth!
God became a man!

Shepherds and wise men traveled far, this Holy Child to see...
Fully God, yet fully man. He came for you and me.
For God's perfect Will.

This child was sent for every man, woman, boy and girl...
To be the ruler of our hearts and Savior of the world.
For God's purpose to Fulfill!

And this is the True meaning of Christmas to share with everyone,
For God so loved the world, that He gave His Only Son!

The Visitor

One cold, dark and windy night, a knock came upon my door...
An older man was standing there, whom I had never seen before.
It was the night of Christmas Eve, so I decided to let him in...
He smiled at me and said hello, as if he were my friend.

He said ... "I bring good news to you, on this blessed night"...
"Jesus our Savior has been born, He is the Son of Light".
"And we should all be celebrating", he went on to say...
"For in the city of Bethlehem, is where the baby lay."

'Now, wait a minute" I interrupted, "How can this be so?'
'Since that happened in the past, centuries ago.'
"Oh no", he argued with me, "For you don't understand,"
"I bring good news to you this night," which shall be for every land."

"Come with me and you will see, the sleeping Holy Child."
Then he reached out his hand, so gentle and so mild,
Now, I thought this guy was very confused and just a touch insane,
I was ready to throw him out the door, but then he called my name.

'How do you know my name?" I cried, "In what way can this be?'
"I know many things" he said, "But for now come and see",
Then we walked outside, at once he pointed to the sky,
"See the star, so bright it shines, to the blindest eye".

'What star?' I said, 'I cannot see a thing!'
"It's there", the man insisted, "It will lead us to the King."
Then suddenly I heard music, a sweet angelic song,
I turned to tell the old man but found that he was gone.

I never saw this man again, which made me very sad,
Because that Christmas turned out to be, the best I ever had.
Perhaps the man was crazy or a little off his gourd,
But I believe he might have been, an angel from the Lord.

One thing is sure... since that night, that I have to say,
The message that He brought to me, is TRUE this very day.
God became a man for us... to be born one starry eve,
So, ALL would have the chance, of Salvation to receive.

So let us tell the story... of Jesus birth, throughout all the year,
Because the message of Good News, is what everyone should hear.

To Follow the Star

Many years ago, a star shown bright with light,
That guided its followers, through the dark of night.
Shepherds and wise men, traveled very far,
To see God's Holy Gift, led by a star.

High above the trees, the star hung over all,
Twinkling with God's Light, o'er Bethlehem so small.
Such a sight of beauty, a miracle of wonder,
Each year at Christmas, makes me often ponder…

Would I have had the desire, to answer such a call?
Would it have led me, to the tiny stall?
Where Jesus lay so peaceful, asleep in divine rest,
Would I have given treasure, of my very best?

I cannot say what might have been,
For it is now and that was then.
Yet, I have searched to fill my soul…
With desperate vices of no control.

To later find the answers of,
A majestic, wondrous and loving God,
That sent His Son, to redeem my life,
Rescuing me from this world of strife.

And in my life I too have found,
God's Shining Light all around.

Scripture References for Selected Poems
Chapter 11
The Gift of Christmas

The Gift of Christmas	Luke 2: 1-14
A Christmas Encouragement	Isaiah 9: 6-7
Christmas in the Real World	Matthew 1:21
Spreading Tidings	I Peter 3:15
The Perfect Gift	John 14:6
The True Meaning of Christmas	Romans 15:13
The Visitor	Isaiah 7:14
To Follow the Star	Matthew 2: 1-2

The Gift of Christmas

For God so loved the world that he gave his one and only Son, that whoever believes in him shall not perish but have eternal life.

John 3:16

CHAPTER TWELVE

HAVE YOU SEEN JESUS?

Have You Seen Jesus?

Who is Jesus? Is He real? Does He know the pain I feel?
Or was He just a teacher, who was very great?
Who in some way was able to predict my fate?

If He died upon the cross, did he die for me?
Was it to give me a life, so that I might go free?
And some say, he rose up from the dead, I wonder is this true?
For I hear He waits to live, inside of me and you.

These questions use to bother me and I did not understand,
For I had always seen Jesus, as just an ordinary man.

Oh sure, I learned about Him,
When I was very small, but never really felt like,
I had ever heard His Call.

"Believe in Jesus" people would say, "For He's coming back again".
But to trust in someone no one had seen,
I could not comprehend.
Until I looked around me and began to see,
Many people whose lives had, been changed drastically...

For their lives displayed a power, that I could not explain,
As I watched them enter trials, yet their faith in God remained.
Their warmth of compassion, seemed to reach me, with such love,
And I knew that I had found something wonderful,
Perhaps, it came from above?

For these were just simple people, a lot like you and I,
But I sensed a special presence, when one of them walked by...
They seemed to have so much, and I just needed more,
And somehow this touched me, like nothing had before...

Have You Seen Jesus?

So in wanting something better and needing a way out,
I decided to give Jesus, the benefit of the doubt.
I got down on my knees and bowed my head to start,
And then I sincerely asked, Jesus, in my heart.

And now I tell you something, was different that very night,
For all the darkness of my life, had turned into His Light.
And now I know that He is real and not lying somewhere dead,
For I had seen the Risen Christ, like everyone had said.

Oh maybe not visually, but I saw Him just the same,
And though the wind howled that night,
I know I heard Him call my name.

Such amazing love like His, could not have compared,
And I no longer had to ask, if Jesus really cared.

Perhaps you are just like me and you don't know what to do.
Maybe you're asking yourself, if what I say is true?
But talk to Jesus, He is there, just give Him a try,
For on a cross He took our place and He chose to die.

And He is not just a body that is lying in a grave.
He is the Risen Christ and you He wants to save.
And if you will ask Him in your heart, there He'll always be,
And you will one day go to live, with Him eternally.

Then you will see Jesus and there will be no doubt,
That He is indeed the Risen Christ that I have told you about.

Don't Come Here! (A Message from Hell)

Don't come here, go away, there is darkness everywhere,
And I can see, you are headed, to this place of despair.
You think that you, have plenty of time, I used to think that too!
But now I burn with others, and there's nothing I can do.

Don't turn away from God's call, it may be your last,
Ask Him to save your human soul and please do it fast.
I've heard some people warn you, about this place I'm in,
But you laugh and snicker, with all your lying friends.

Let me tell you something, I have friends like that with me,
And they don't care about my fate, or endless agony.
But I can see that you're not interested, in what I have to say,
Because you are so much like me, in every kind of way.

So that's okay, don't you listen, to the message that I tell,
And then someday, when it's too late, I WILL SEE YOU HERE IN HELL.

Finding Tomorrow

How do we find a new tomorrow?
When we're trapped inside the past...
How do we find hope?
When our dreams did not last...

When everything is gone,
How can we find more?
That will lead us to something better,
Than what we had before.

Finding a new tomorrow,
Is easy to be found.
When we go to Jesus,
And we lay our burdens down.

So let us search for God's Love...
That will never go away,
Then we'll find that a new tomorrow,
Will have become our Joy today.

God's Watching

Through hills of sorrow,
Through tunnels of despair.

On roads of darkness,
I know He's there.

And someday when He comes again,
I know my heart is cleansed from sin.

Then I'll be walking on a golden bay,
Hoping and praying, I'll see You one day.

So if you want to see me too,
Call on Jesus, He's waiting for YOU!

Hey It's Me

Hey it's me, and I wish you could see,
Everything I told you about, is as I expected it would be.

Heaven is so wonderful, and there's a lot to do,
I wish you could be a part, of everything so new.

It's exciting and beautiful but most importantly,
I am living up here with Jesus, for eternity.

You should see the pearly gates, and the tree of life,
And everyone is happy here, there isn't a bit of strife.

You wouldn't believe the joy, I feel, that I have waited for so long,
And all the bliss of this Glorious Place, will go on and on and on....

I am so glad I accepted Christ in my heart, many years ago,
And I wish that you were here, because I love you so.

If only you had accepted Him too! Then we would be together,
But you didn't and the choice you made was unfortunately, FOREVER!

Identity

Who am I? What is my purpose?
Does anyone care for me?
What do I have to give to share?
Are there any guarantees?

The world says it is fame and stardom.
Is this my destiny? Maybe as a humanitarian,
I could find where I'm supposed to be…
Perhaps, fortune holds the key?

Maybe its thrills and living on the edge?
With no fear you see.
For I have heard others boast of this revelry.
Maybe "this" I can foresee, I'm searching desperately.
And yet… I can't help but think there's more…
And I'm waiting patiently,

For life to have meaning and unmistakably,
Lead me to answers justifiably,
As soon as possible, hopefully…

Perhaps the essence of life, is not to live recklessly,
Or live it to the fullest, so vicariously,
But to give some serious thought, of an eternity.

Now maybe others will disagree,
But this is about me…

Because I have heard of a Savior, who can set me free,
Who suffered for my sin, in endless agony
Yet the hold of death, failed miserably,
Because Jesus arose victoriously!

So it makes sense abundantly!

For me to pray to Him and fall on my knees,
Asking for God's Forgiveness and Mercy…
To the very ONE, who undeniably,
Holds my future and my Identity.

Live it Up!

You've heard Jesus calling you, as He knocked upon your door,
But you chose to turn Him down, just like you've done before.
And since being a child of God, is not what you want to be,
Then this world is the only, part of Heaven you will see.

So live it up my friend! Go on and celebrate,
Because one day for you, it will be too late.
You eat drink and be merry, without any kind of fear,
But you had better hurry, because the day is drawing near.

For one day when Jesus returns, and the time is at hand,
He will be the one, who will be in command.
And when He asks you, why you turned Him away,
Then to Him, what will you say?
The party will be over, as you hold your bitter cup,
For your life will be finished, and all lived up!

R.S.V.P.

This is an invitation, to join us one and all,
For a celebration, when we hear the trumpet call.

This celebration will be, the greatest and the best,
We shall live with our King, in Perfect Peace and Rest.

It's the party of a Lifetime, when all shall finally see,
Jesus as the King of Kings, in all His Royalty.

Many will begin, to cast crowns at His feet,
And at the Marriage Supper, we shall sit down to eat.

You too are invited, to celebrate this Glorious day,
But you will need to make, a decision without delay.

The time is drawing nearer, for this Holy Preparation,
If you expect to be there, you need a Reservation.

In the Lambs Book of Life, is where your name must be,
So if you plan to attend, you must R. S. V. P.

(Receive Salvation via Prayer)

Sacrificing

In this world we live in, there is a lot of,
Sacrificing and doing without, for the ones we love.

And even though we forfeit, without a second thought,
We don't sacrifice for the One, who really gave a lot.

You say that being a Christian and living life so new,
Isn't the kind of sacrificing, that you plan to do?

You don't want to give up, on things that pertain to sin,
But what you don't realize, God wants to be your friend.

You'll have a place to live, when your life is through,
It will either be Heaven or Hell, it's really up to you.

But friend would you consider, the sacrifice of all,
God sent His Son to die, so that we might hear His call.

This to me is special, Him being sent down for man,
He really must love us, to take such a stand.

So, in seeing how much He sacrificed, it seems only just,
That we could sacrifice a little, for all He's done for us.

Ski Patrol

Sometimes on the mountain, you will often see,
A rescue effort taking place, in answer to a plea.

It might be that a skier chose, the wrong trail to ski,
Or perhaps someone is injured and needs help desperately.

So the ski patrol goes out and rescues those in distress,
Bringing them down the mountain, with safety at its best.

We too are born into this world and we start out on a trail,
Headed for destruction always bound for Hell.

But God offers us salvation, through a second birth,
For He sent His only Son, for everyone on earth.

And those who call upon His name, shall be saved from death,
To live life eternally, with peace and happiness.

The Big Screen

One night I dreamed I was in Heaven, and it was judgment day,
Where millions of people stood in line, to face their grim dismay.

So when it was my turn, I felt confident before the Lord,
For I was a Christian, and I expected a great reward.

Until the Lord showed me a big screen, that was suspended in the sky,
And everything I had encountered in life, started flashing by.

All the times I turned Him away, or disobeyed shamelessly,
Now was showing on this big screen, for everyone to see.

I just stood there in a dumbfounded way, for I could not deny a thing,
Because every single part of my life, was now showing on this screen.

I felt such shame and dishonor, but what was I to do,
For all the dark secrets of my life, everyone now knew.

I wanted to escape all of my guilt, but there was nowhere to run,
For I could not change or even hide, what I had or had not done.

It was then I awoke from my dream, with swollen tear filled eyes,
Under great conviction, for I begin to realize.

That if my life would one day be revealed, for everyone to see,
Then I must start living my life, the way that it should be.

For one day all will stand before God and all will stand alone,
To give account for all they've done, all that was right and wrong.

And on that day of reckoning, there at the judgment seat,
Will we have but one reward, to lay at Jesus feet?

The Knock at My Door

Once I heard a knock, at my hearts door,
And a man named Jesus, whom I'd never seen before,
Was patiently waiting, to come inside,
But His Love, I pushed aside.

Then there was another day,
I heard the same knock, in the same way,
Once again it was Jesus, standing there,
But I did not let Him in, nor did I care.

Finally, a third knock, did I hear,
And again it was Jesus, with falling tears,
Begging to come in, and save my soul,
Wanting me to give Him, complete control.

I nearly opened the door that time,
But for some reason, I changed my mind,
Now I don't hear, that knocking plea...
Because Jesus is no longer, waiting for me.

I turned Him away, like all the times before,
When I didn't open, my hearts closed door.

The Search

Your questions without answers, with disbelief and doubt,
Sometimes leave you paralyzed, not seeing a way out.

Different views and opinions, you hear from everyone,
Only confuse your thinking, when all's been said and done.

Feeling down and lonely, as if all hope is gone,
And though some good things happen, you still can't carry on.

People reaching everywhere, mile after mile,
Yet it seems they do not care, because you do not see their smile.

Your family shows they love you, as they stretch out their hand,
But deep down you still feel rejected, because you do not understand.

You sometimes scream and yell because you're mad at yourself,
And inside things are moving fast, though your life is on the shelf.

But you are not crazy, nor have you lost your mind,
You're just concerned and worried that you're running out of time.

You're searching for something special, that you never had,
And you can't seem to find it, so it makes you very mad.

But the search has been over, a long time you see,
When Jesus came to die for you, on a hill called Calvary.

And by trusting in Him fully and accepting Him today,
You will find what you've been searching for is just a prayer away.

And though every problem you're going through, may not disappear,
Jesus will walk by your side and dry your every tear.

For Jesus Christ is waiting, to be your closest friend,
For when you call on Him, your search will come to an end.

The Two Crowds

Many years ago there lived two crowds of people,
That walked upon the earth every day.

There was one crowd, who would always follow Jesus Christ,
And another crowd who turned Him away.

The followers of Christ, loved and adored Him,
And believed the words that He said.

But the crowd that followed after all other things,
Only laughed at Him instead.

Then one day the hateful crowd, grew jealous,
And crucified Jesus on the cross.

And it seemed the crowd that loved Him,
Had suffered a great loss...

But then He arose from the grave, in which death had destroyed,
And the crowd that had followed after Him, was glad and overjoyed.

Today, the same two crowds exist, to which crowd do you belong?
Are you a follower of Jesus Christ? Or do you follow after the wrong.

For one day when He comes again, the two crowds will He see,
Then Jesus will ask the crowds of two, "Who follows after me"?

And both crowds will say "I DO LORD", but one will not be true,
And He will say to the false crowd, "Depart I never knew you".

Then Jesus will take His crowd to Heaven, where His Love will prevail,
And the other crowd will be left alone, to spend eternity in HELL.

The Ultimate Challenge or Fatal Mistake

The green trail is the easiest to ski,
But somewhat hard for people like me.
The blue trail is more difficult they say.
A higher level in skiing today.
But the ultimate challenge is higher still.
The black diamond is the most dangerous trail,
Its mountain is steep with cliffs so high.
It's a dare, to every skier that passes by.

The thrill, the feeling to ski its side,
The risk, the story that some, have died.
Others no one can persuade,
To try to fake such a charade.
But the one who can ski it with control,
Knows the danger that it holds.
A beginner would never, attempt such an act,
If he were not a good skier, without all the facts,

Yet people are playing with a danger so real,
Flirting with Satan because of the thrill.
He allures them to thinking, that they can have power,
Yet their life can be snuffed out, in only one hour.
They are living their lives, without the Holy One,
As they jump into sinful desires of fun.
But if they do not accept Jesus, then they will all see,
Their fatal mistake of destiny.

Scripture References for Selected Poems
Chapter 12
Have You Seen Jesus

Have You Seen Jesus	John 3: 1-21
Don't Come Here!	Luke 16: 19-31
God's Watching	Psalm 139: 7-10
Hey It's Me	John 3: 11-18
Identity	Galatians 2:20
Live It Up	Revelation 22:20
R.S.V.P.	Revelation 19:9
The Big Screen	2 Corinthians 5:10
The Knock at My Door	Revelation 3:20
The Two Crowds	Matthew 7:21-23

The Trusting Time

One Last Plea...

I Hope I See You There!

Suppose that something were to happen to you, and you died suddenly,
Would you know for sure, where you would spend eternity?

Have you ever asked the question, that concerns the heart?
Which will one day determine, where your soul departs.

Perhaps the thought has crossed your mind, though not so seriously,
But friend your time is running out and you must act quickly.

So choose this day whom you will serve, and do not hesitate!
Because one day for you, I'm afraid it will be too late...

And don't put off till tomorrow, what should be done today,
Accept Jesus Christ in your heart, without any more delay.

For He's standing at the door, knocking just for you,
And He will come in right now, if you ask Him to.

So please consider all I've said, and handle your choice with care,
For I know that one day I will be in Heaven, and I hope to see YOU there!

Jesus answered, "I am the way and the truth and the life.
No one comes to the Father except through me. John 14:6

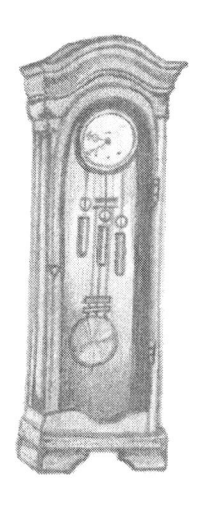

Scripture Verses
One Last Plea
I Hope I See You There

Luke 13:22-28 Jesus went through the towns and villages, teaching as he made his way to Jerusalem. Someone asked him, "Lord, are only a few people going to be saved?" He said to them, "Make every effort to enter through the narrow door, because many, I tell you, will try to enter and will not be able to. Once the owner of the house gets up and closes the door, you will stand outside knocking and pleading, `Sir, open the door for us.' "But he will answer, `I don't know you or where you come from.' "Then you will say, `We ate and drank with you, and you taught in our streets.' "But he will reply, `I don't know you or where you come from. Away from me, all you evildoers!' "There will be weeping there, and gnashing of teeth, when you see Abraham, Isaac and Jacob and all the prophets in the kingdom of God, but you yourselves thrown out.

Hebrews 9:27-28 Just as man is destined to die once, and after that to face judgment, so Christ was sacrificed once to take away the sins of many people; and he will appear a second time, not to bear sin, but to bring salvation to those who are waiting for him.

James 2:19 You believe that there is one God. Good! Even the demons believe that—and shudder.

I John 5:11-13 And this is the testimony: God has given us eternal life, and this life is in his Son. Whoever has the Son has life; whoever does not have the Son of God does not have life.

An Invitation For You...

A Sinner's Prayer

Oh Lord, I know I am a sinner, this I realize,
And I've heard that You forgive all sins, despite the size.

So I'm asking Your forgiveness, for everything I've done,
And I want You to be my Savior, now while I'm still young.

And now after living in sin, not knowing what to do,
I'm ready to leave the world behind, and follow after You.

So now please come into my heart, and rescue me from sin,
And let me be of service to You, and know You more.... Amen.

If you declare with your mouth, "Jesus is Lord," and believe in your heart that God raised him from the dead, you will be saved. For it is with your heart that you believe and are justified, and it is with your mouth that you profess your faith and are saved. Romans 10:9-10

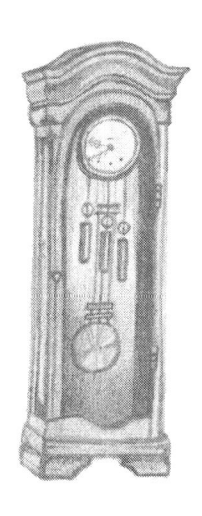

Scripture Verses
An Invitation For You
A Sinner's Prayer

Romans 3:23 *For all have sinned and fall short of the glory of God.*

John 3:16 *For God so loved the world that he gave his one and only Son, that whoever believes in him shall not perish but have eternal life.*

Romans 6:22-23 *For the wages of sin is death, but the gift of God is eternal life in Christ Jesus our Lord.*

Ephesians 2:8-9 *For it is by grace you have been saved, through faith--and this not from yourselves, it is the gift of God-- not by works, so that no one can boast.*

The Trusting Time

(P.S.),

A few disclaimers about this book

In the process of getting this book put together, I consulted with a few people, including one editor. Poetry is not edited the way most books are by most editors. Poetry can vary in its style, mood and format. It is with my style and preference that I like for my poetry to rhyme. You have probably already noticed three things... 1) Poems in this book are simple, clear and to the point. 2) I can tell you that this book has been reviewed numerous times by several people and it still might have some imperfections in it related to grammar, punctuation, rhythm or format. I hope that if you do find one that it won't stop or distract you from getting the real message of this book. This book is about God, for God and I like to believe that He is more Powerful than any comma, dash or dot. 3) Another thing you may have noticed is that I tend to capitalize letters a lot more than most people. This is my way of bringing more awareness to what is being said and its importance as well as to show the reverence for who God is.

A few childhood memories: The earliest memory I have as a child was sometime in the year of **1966**. I was around the age of three and half years old and was sandwiched between my mom and my grandmother with my aunt on the other side of her, as we sat on a pew listening to a heavy set woman with a soprano voice singing... an old hymn called "Are You Ready". My mom, grandmother and aunt were all crying... It was my great grandmother's funeral. She was the woman who was responsible for handing down a spiritual legacy to all of us. I didn't know it then and it is difficult to explain now, but even though I don't remember knowing her while she was alive, she has made an indelible mark on my life. Sarah Angeline Bunton, (although everyone knew her as Ma), would first earn a place in my heart and eventually a poem in my collection- ***Ma***.

I do not know the exact date and age that I accepted Jesus as my Savior but I DO remember the moment as if it were yesterday. I went down the aisle during a Sunday night church service while the hymn "Have Thine Own Way" was playing. I didn't understand everything then as a small child but I knew that Jesus loved me and I knew I wanted to give my heart to Him. I have to say this is where my writing career started because it wasn't long after that when I wrote my very first poem- ***God's Watching***.

When I was young I wrote poem after poem. Several poems were written between the year of **1976 and 1982**. These were very basic poems such as: ***A Sinner's Prayer, A Christian Prayer, Sacrificing*** and ***The Lighthouse***. I had no idea then, but God was carving out a ministry for me that would encourage others with His Love and Truth.

The only time that I was ever graded on a poem in school was when I was in my senior year of high school. I received a D+ on it. I was so upset and discouraged that I wanted to throw it away and never write again! However, I showed it to my mom and after taking a closer look she discovered that other than a few misspelled words, the main remarks were about the teacher's personal belief and did not reflect on the editing at all. The remarks she made indicated that she did not believe the content that I was writing about and so she had based my grade on her own personal opinion. I took the grade and never argued with her because somewhere deep down I felt like God still had a purpose for me even though I wasn't treated fairly at the time. The poem was called- ***The Crucifixion***.

My senior year of high school (**class of 1982**) was no different than any other's senior year, full of anticipation to graduate and full of hesitation for what lied ahead. There was however, one major highlight of that year and that was I had my first poem published. It was published in my church's newspaper. It was on orange paper and I still have it. *The poem-* ***The Sparrow*** is one of my favorites to this very day.

Once I graduated I never forgot about the poem that was given such a terrible grade because of a teacher's own opinion. I often struggled with confidence when writing because of that unfair grade. So, you could imagine my surprise when that same poem **The Crucifixion** was later accepted and published in my town's newspaper in **1987**. The only problem was that when I submitted it I happened to have a huge eye patch over my left eye (due to an eye abrasion) and I believed that they just felt sorry for me. Yet, I would still bravely submit new poems to the newspaper and they accepted and published them all, over the next few years. However, because of that one bad experience with the teacher, it would be years before I was convinced that I indeed had a talent.

A few noteworthy moments: In the spring of **1989** I decided to submit one poem-- **Even the Flowers Knew** for a poetry contest. I remember praying to God that I didn't care if I won the contest but I just wanted to know that He had touched someone's heart with that poem. I won an honorable mention certificate along with a personal letter from the editor who told me that the poem meant a lot to her. I framed the certificate and now it hangs in my office at home.

In **1990** I met this guy (now my husband, Phil) who shared with me how he had been hurt many times by past relationships. Shortly after we started dating I wrote a poem for him called- **The Heart Mender** and framed it as a gift for him. It also hangs on the wall in our office at home.

In **1991** my life was forever changed when my grandfather died suddenly one December day. Even after all these years I still think about him and miss him very much. I heard that he had been ill and I was asked to go and visit him. I was caught up with life and failed to make it a priority. I guess I believed that I had all the time in the world but ... one Sunday morning that time ran out. The thought of not visiting him or saying goodbye has haunted me for years and still haunts me now. The poem- **Pa** was a tribute to him and it was read at his funeral. The best memory that I have of my grandfather is when he would take me to Dairy Queen and order me a chocolate malt extra malt. I have many memories like this one and they make me smile.

During the time of **1991** through **1993** I wrote poems about being single and how God was working in my life. The poem that stands out to me during this time was- **It's Never Too Late for Love.** Although I secretly hoped early on that Phil and I would one day be married, I also knew that God had a purpose for me while I was still single. This poem ministered to me as I waited on God's Timing and His Will. I hope it does the same for other single adults as well.

In April of **1996** I submitted another poem in a poetry contest called-- **View from the Top.** This poem was written after I had actually ridden in the ski lift for the very first time. If you have ever gone skiing you know that the silence can be deafening. At that time I could almost hear God whisper to me and I felt His Peace in a wonderful way. I only won honorable mention but it was printed with hundreds of other poems in a book.

In the year **2000**-**Soul Mate from Heaven** was written, another poem that I wrote for Phil. This time it was on our third wedding anniversary. He loved it and it now sits in a frame on his desk at work.

During **2001-2008** I was very involved with encouragement ministries. Some of these ministries were in churches and would provide a platform for me to encourage others through a few of the older poems I had written. Other encouragement opportunities came through my personal ministries, outside of the church walls-- where I wrote less poetry and more devotionals for newsletters.

Sometime during the year of **2009** my grandmother, who has been my spiritual mentor since I was a child, had to be placed in a nursing home. It has been extremely difficult for me and my family as we have had to watch such a strong woman of faith slowly lose herself in dementia. At the writing of this book she doesn't recognize me as her granddaughter but she still enjoys my visits. The poem **Trapped Inside** is about how my family and I have had to cope during these moments with her. In years past "Grannie" would often help critique and encourage me with the poems that I wrote. I usually would not share a newly written poem with anyone until I had shared it with her first. I miss this part of my life with her the most because she was my biggest fan. My favorite memory I have of her is when I had moved in with her after my grandfather had died. She would wait up for me after a date, church or singles activity and listen to me tell her about every sordid detail. As I was talking she would sometimes go to the refrigerator and pull out a surprise bowl of homemade chocolate pudding.

By the fall of **2009** I had all but stopped writing, except for an occasional seasonal newsletter once in a while. It was also in that same year that I began noticing I was having a lot more achiness and pain than usual and this would usher in a big life change. I was diagnosed with Fibromyalgia. At first my diagnosis was only a mild one but recently it has increased tremendously. This condition often makes me feel like I have worked out extra hard or I just feel bruised all over. I am constantly in a state of chronic pain, fatigue and weakness. However, God has helped me to deal with this difficulty by expressing it through poems such as ***In the Suffering***, ***In the Clearing***, ***The Constant***, ***Point to Him*** and ***Troubled Thoughts***. These along with several other new poems in Chapter 6, were written from a personal perspective of trusting God whether in time of pain, depression, fear, abandonment or grief.

In the spring of **2010** God began preparing me for my biggest venture yet. He used two good friends of mine to grab my attention, so that I would consider writing a book. One friend, Megan Breedlove, announced her plan to write and publish a devotional book. She is now published and her book "Manna for Moms" is available in stores. The other friend, Michelle Dietrich, shared with me one summer ago that she also was writing a book. She is writing a Christian fiction book "In the Gap "and hopes to have it out soon. I wanted to give a shout out to these two dear friends because they are part of the journey that led up to how God started the process of (me writing) this book.

In the winter of **2011**, after a difficult summer and spring of various troubles and trials… my husband and I decided to escape to the mountains of New Mexico, for a little rest and relaxation as well as spiritual renewal. There as we were surrounded by majestic mountains, snow covered ground and God's Presence… He beckoned me back to writing and confirmed in many different ways, the calling to write my own book. For the first time in a long time I started seeing myself as a writer again and becoming a published author!

In the summer of **2011** I began working on the book and God began slowly guiding me to choose a title. Since I wanted to name the book after a poem, I knew that there were many to choose from but as God continued to intertwine my whole life with all of the good and bad, He revealed the theme of the book to be bigger than the title itself. My final selection was a simple poem about trusting and it soon became the whole precipice for the book itself and the title- ***The Trusting Time.*** This poem was written several years earlier during a time when I was fighting a small bout of depression. I wrote it while sitting on the beach in Destin, Florida. The ocean has always been another hot spot where I like to get my inspiration. Whenever we vacation there my favorite thing to do, other than writing-- is look for seashells.

God blessed me with the inspiration of writing 26 new poems for this collection. They are: ***Beautiful Lullaby***, ***Expressions***, ***Honest Worship***, ***My Constant***, ***Poured Out***, ***Prayer for Contentment***, ***God's Creation***, ***Fear and Fret Not***, ***In the Clearing***, ***In the Suffering***, ***Panic Attack***, ***Point to Him***, ***Trapped Inside***, ***Troubled Thoughts***, ***When Bad Things Happen***, ***The Folded Flag***, ***More Than Stories***, ***Simple Poems***, ***New Year's Resolution***, ***The Lives We Touch Are Many***, ***Daniel***, ***David and Goliath***, ***Lunch Break***, ***Piggy Bank***, ***Identity*** and ***R.S.V.P***.

The new poem ***The Folded Flag*** was the last poem written for this collection. I wrote it during the week of the 10 year anniversary of 9/11. My heart was heavy for the men and women in military that are still serving in the war against terrorism. I also have a fond respect for all those who have served in previous wars.

A few interesting facts: This is not the first time I have written a book. I have actually written seven others. They were compilations of the older poems. In the past I simply would get them copyrighted and then would take them to the local printer. They were never professionally published until now.

Several of the older poems and their titles have been changed or revised, either in content or their titles. *Some editing can have that kind of "positive" effect on writers.* I have been extremely selective with what God wanted me to use and/or change about each poem. So if you happen to take note of an older poem or two with a different title or content that is why.

All photos and illustrations have been carefully selected to continue the theme throughout this book and send the repetitive message for each chapter, as they complement each other.

The name "April Sky" originated from a request for me to come up with a pen name by a group of editors, for a submission in a poetry contest. So, I decided to pick something easy like my birthday month and an element of God's creation. To this day it makes me think about an Easter morning in April whenever I hear the name.

There are many poems that I like but my all-time favorite poems are-- **_The Sparrow_** and **_Have You Seen Jesus_**. "The Sparrow" has a simple message of what happens when we leave God or we cease to put Him first in our lives while the poem "Have You Seen Jesus" expresses my heart for the lost. These two poems touch me every time I read them.

My poetry writing was inspired by three famous poets: **_Dr. Seuss, Edgar Allen Poe,_** and **_Helen Steiner Rice._**

A hint of Dr. Seuss' influence can be seen in my poems-- **_A Change of Heart_**, and **_The Visitor_**, while a darker influence of Edgar Allen Poe can be seen in my poems-- **_Don't Come Here_**, **_Live it Up_** and **_Knock at My Door_**.

Helen Steiner Rice's influence offered a more inspirational touch and can be seen in my poems **_Prayer of Praise, Just Remember, His Unchanging Love_** and **_The True Meaning of Christmas_**.

For anyone who knows me, it goes without saying that my favorite author has been and continues to be **_Max Lucado_**. He doesn't write poetry but his writings are very inspirational to me and others all over the world. I have been influenced by him with the devotionals that I write. My husband and I had the pleasure of meeting him at his church in San Antonio, Texas several years ago. I love his books and have almost every one of them.

A few final acknowledgements: As the next part of my journey begins as an author, I first want to mention of how blessed I am that God has allowed my dreams to come true. These poems were once just collecting dust in my office drawer. Yet, God's specialty is taking what is old, dusty and forgotten, and making it new, shiny and memorable. He has done that for these poems, this book and more importantly my life.

I also want to mention how thankful I am to God for my husband. Phil has been my manager, editor, computer tech and co-laborer during this entire journey of getting this book published. I truly could not have done it without his sacrifice of time, encouragement and patience. God used this book to encourage him personally as he was helping me to get it all together. By the way, if you ever get the chance to meet him in person you will see the better half of me ☺

I must also note that my two cats Abbie and Daisy have been an extra special blessing by God while writing this book. They have often been right beside me lending their support, while God worked. Abbie has been present with a peaceful demeanor while Daisy has added her own flair by chewing on some of the rejected remnants of this project, to her delight.

Last, but certainly not least—I want to mention how blessed I am to you, the reader of this book. Yes, you! Thank you for choosing to read "this" book. Thank you for placing this book in an area of your home where others can enjoy it. Thank you for allowing God to touch your life through the poetry of my life, in order to make your life poetic for Him!

For I know the plans I have for you," declares the LORD, "plans to prosper you and not to harm you, plans to give you hope and a future. Jeremiah 29:11

The Trusting Time

Alphabetical Index of Poems

A Change of Heart	21
A Child's Smile	165
A Christian's Prayer	57
A Christmas Encouragement	185
A Friend Like You	151
A Hope for Spring	73
A Joy for Summer	74
A Peace for Fall	75
A Prayer for Grief	58
A Saviors Love for You	3
A Single Red Rose	23
A Single's Prayer	59
A Sinner's Prayer	216
A Tiny Little Light	166
A Valentine of Praise	89
Acknowledgement of His Glory	x
Acknowledging His Holiness	43
Afraid of the Dark	167
America's Last Hope	125
Angels Are Here	90
As We Stand	91
Astray	22
Autograph of Love	2
Beautiful Lullaby	24
Blessing Before Bitterness	25
Christmas in the Real World	186
Commitment of Love	26
Coronation at Calvary	4
Daniel	168
David and Goliath	169
Don't Come Here! (A Message from Hell)	198
Even the Flowers Knew	5
Even the Tree's Bow	76
Every Remembrance of You (A Poem of Friendship)	152
Expressions	42
Faith for Winter	77
Fear and Fret Not	92
Fear of Heights	94
Finding Tomorrow	199
Final Touches	137

Alphabetical Index of Poems (continued)

For the Graduate	153
Forgiveness of His Own	27
Freedom for All	126
Genuine Love	138
God's Country	127
God's Creation	78
God's Greenhouse	170
God's Plan	95
God's Watching	200
God's Way	96
Grief (The Mysterious Gift)	97
Have You Seen Jesus	196
Heaven	171
Heaven Presents "Jesus"	44
Heaven's Love	6
Hey It's Me	201
His Unchanging Love	79
Hog Heaven	139
Honest Worship	45
I Cannot Feel	98
I Hope I See You There!	214
Identity	202
In God's Hand	140
In the Clearing	99
In the Suffering	100
It's Never Too Late for Love	28
JESUS	172
Just a Kid	164
Just Remember	101
Just to Say	102
Lesson of Love	29
Little Butterflies	173
Live it Up	203
Look Up! "Broken-Hearts"	30
Looking Beyond	103
Love Throughout the Ages	7
Lullaby Prayer	174
Lunch Break	175
Ma	154
Many Glimpses of God's Glory	80
Mercy	31

Alphabetical Index of Poems (continued)

Momma Tells Me	176
More than Stories	136
My Constant	46
My Prayer of Praise	60
My Wedding Day	8
Never Thirst Again	9
New Year's Resolution	155
Out of the Nest	141
Pa	156
Panic Attack	104
Piggy Bank	177
Pity Party	105
Point to Him	106
Poured Out	47
Prayer for a Friend	62
Prayer for Contentment	63
Prayer for Faith	64
Prayer of Forgiveness	65
Prayer Time	66
Prayers Down the Hall	61
Prepare Me for Eternity	48
Quiet Time with God	49
R.S.V.P.	204
Removing the Masks	142
Returning to the Valley	107
Romance Made in Heaven	32
Sacrificing	205
Sacrificing Comfort, Accepting Change	33
Sand Castles	108
Seeds of Encouragement	81
Seminary Student's Prayer	67
Shadows	10
Simple Poems	150
Sinner's Prayer	216
Ski Patrol	206
Spiritual Sight	82
Spreading Tidings	188
Storms of Life	83
Take Another Look America	124
Taking a Moment	11
Teach Me	157

Alphabetical Index of Poems (continued)

Telling the Truth	180
Thank You	158
That Special Someone	34
The Big Screen	207
The Crucifixion	12
The Devil	178
The Empty Playground	128
The Folded Flag	129
The Gift of Christmas	184
The Great Ecstasy	50
The Heart Mender	20
The Heavenly King	13
The Hollow Heart	109
The Knock at My Door	208
The Lamb and the Wolf	179
The Lighthouse	143
The Lives We Touch Are Many	159
The Love You Can't Replace	35
The Main Attraction	14
The Perfect Gift	187
The Power of Prayer	56
The Safest Place	110
The Search	209
The Silver Years	160
The Snowy Surface	15
The Sparrow	144
The Sunshine	84
The Traveler and the Follower	145
The True Meaning of Christmas	189
The Trusting Time	88
The Two Crowds	210
The Ultimate Challenge or Fatal Mistake	211
The Unanswered Prayer	68
The Visitor	190
The Wall	36
Timing the Waves	51
To Encourage Others	111
To Follow the Star	191
To Suffer Rejection	112
Trapped Inside	113
Troubled Thoughts	114

Alphabetical Index of Poems (continued)

True American Way	
Trust in God	115
Victorious Over All	52
View from the Top	72
What Will It Take	131
When Bad Things Happen	116
When the Vows Have Been Broken	117
Why Do Bad Things Happen?	118
Windows of Light	119
Words Cannot Express	120
Yesterday's Miracle	16
You Knew Me Lord	37

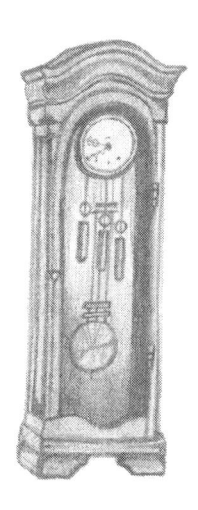

ABOUT THE AUTHOR

Jodie Mitchell was born and raised in Texas. She is a former Elk and graduate of Burleson High School.

Although she is new to the circle of self-published authors, her first poem "The Sparrow" was published in a church's newsletter in 1982. In the past and as a home town writer she has had poems published in the town newspapers of both Burleson and Crowley.

One poem "View From the Top" can be found in the publications of the National Library of Poetry (1996).

She currently lives in Crowley, Texas with her husband Phil, her two cats Abbie and Daisy and two dogs Koda and Kenai. She and her husband are the proud aunt and uncle of several nieces and nephews in Texas, Oklahoma and Australia. She and her husband presently serve at and are members of Christ Chapel Bible Church.

When she isn't writing poetry she is writing devotionals, mentoring women and praying for others. She has been involved with encouragement ministries for thirteen years and currently she is the Spiritual Care Encourager/Coordinator for April Sky Ministries, which she and her husband minister to others through their website.

To learn more about April Sky check out the website www.aprilsky.net .

Made in the USA
Charleston, SC
15 October 2011